Self-evaluation in Physical Education: Developing the process

Gillian Salter-Smith
John Pearson

association for
Physical
Education

baalpe

ISBN-13: 978-1-905540-06-8
ISBN-10: 1-905540-06-X

Authors
Gillian Salter-Smith
John Pearson

After completing the self-evaluation continuing professional development exercises, delegates should use their professional development record to demonstrate the impact of their self-evaluation professional development in the workplace. You may then wish to submit your portfolio of evidence for Accredited Prior Experimental Learning (APEL) which will count towards a higher qualification at any HEI.

The British Association of Advisers and Lecturers in Physical Education (baalpe) and the Physical Education Association UK (PEA UK) dissolved in April 2006. The Association for Physical Education (afPE) is the new physical education subject association for all professionals with appropriate qualifications in physical education, sport and dance.

British Association of Advisers and Lecturers
in Physical Education (baalpe)
University College Worcester
Henwick Grove
Worcester WR2 6AJ

Tel: 01905-855 584
Fax: 01905-855 594
Email: admin.baalpe@worc.ac.uk
Website: www.baalpe.org

Association for Physical Education
Building 25
London Road
Reading RG1 5AQ

Tel: 0118-378 6240
Fax: 0118-378 6242
Website: www.afpe.org.uk

Published on behalf of baalpe and afPE by

Coachwise Business Solutions

Coachwise Business Solutions
Coachwise Ltd
Chelsea Close
Off Amberley Road
Armley
Leeds LS12 4HP

Tel: 0113-231 1310
Fax: 0113-231 9606
Email: enquiries@coachwisesolutions.co.uk
Website: www.coachwisesolutions.co.uk

050061

About the Authors

Gillian Salter-Smith is an experienced physical education teacher, inspector and trainer. She is an additional inspector for Ofsted, currently employed by a regional inspection services provider. Gillian is also a qualified trainer for Ofsted and has written about and led training on inspecting physical education for Ofsted inspectors. Prior to September 2005, she worked as a team inspector (for 12 years) and as a registered inspector (for five years) on Ofsted inspections of schools. She has led baalpe and Ofsted training on self-evaluation for leaders of physical education in schools. As well as being head of department in a comprehensive school, she has been an advisory teacher for Cumbria LEA and worked in teacher training at Leeds Metropolitan University and Charlotte Mason College, Lancaster.

John Pearson has been involved with physical education for over 35 years as a teacher, head of department, advisory teacher, head of an ILEA school sports centre, county adviser and independent consultant. He was the first recipient of the Gerald Murray Award of PEA UK and was elected a fellow in 1983. He was also the first individual recipient of a Professional Development Board (PDB) for PE Providers' Licence. He has been involved nationally as a national lead trainer for the PESS CPD programme. In addition, he has been involved in leading training on inspecting physical education for Ofsted inspectors, and has also led training for leaders of physical education on self-evaluation in schools for baalpe and Ofsted. His other interests at regional and national level relate to training and the development of performance management in schools and centres.

Preface

Self-evaluation in Physical Education: Developing the process is an essential resource for all personnel who are involved in the process of evaluating the standards and quality of physical education in schools. It is a key tool for those involved in the leadership and management of physical education as they and their colleagues lead the drive for improvement in the subject, by ensuring teaching is inspiring, the curriculum is innovative and learners are motivated and engaged.

Nationally, the education agenda, particularly those elements associated with inspection and review, has placed self-evaluation at the heart of that process. Ofsted make the point that 'schools that do not know themselves cannot adequately manage themselves'. The acid tests of self-evaluation focus on involving all stakeholders in the process, using a range of telling evidence to answer questions about pupils' learning, achievement and development. The evidence collected should recognise success and inform improvement.

Ultimately, self-evaluation should lead to actions that promote standards and improve the quality of the learning experiences for all pupils. This resource adopts a detailed step-by-step approach through the process of self-evaluation based on the Ofsted framework and using a wide range of case studies drawn from primary, special and secondary schools, and provides clear guidance on good practice. Any improvement needs to begin with an unrelenting emphasis on learning and the impact teaching has on it. The lessons on the DVD provide the opportunity for a considered, reflective analysis of teaching and its impact on learning. This aspect of the resource alone can prompt discussion and dialogue between colleagues, particularly when answering the question, 'what constitutes best practice?'. The resource gives guidance with specific tasks to be undertaken over a period of time, so that personnel can make clear, qualitative judgements based on standards and levels of achievement. Such accurate judgements regarding teaching and learning, and leadership and management, are crucial for identifying how improvements can be achieved.

This is the definitive resource for self-evaluation in physical education. I urge all colleagues involved in the teaching of physical education to use it to reflect on their practice and ensure all learners enjoy and achieve in physical education. I fully endorse this resource and am in no doubt of the benefit that working through the modules will have on the knowledge, skills and motivation of yourselves and that of your pupils. We know that 'Every Child Matters' (2005), but it is also important to remember that every lesson counts!

Clare Stretch
Senior Inspector, Wirral Local Authority

Contents

Page

Abbreviations   1

Overview   5

National Expectations and Criteria   10

Unit 1: Introduction to Self-evaluation   15

Unit 2: Evaluating Learners' Standards, Achievement,
Personal Development and Well-being in Physical Education   36

Unit 3: Evaluating the Impact of a School's Provision (Especially Teaching and Assessment)
on Pupil's Standards, Achievement, Personal Development and Well-being in Physical Education   67

Unit 4: Evaluating Leadership and Management   91

Appendix 1: Primary School Case Study   118

Appendix 11: Secondary School Case Study   133

Appendix 111: Example of a Completed Self-evaluation Form from Biddick School   152

References   189

Further Reading   190

Acknowledgements

Thank you to the head teacher and class teachers of Years 2 and 6 at East Herrington Primary School, Sunderland, for being involved in the production of lesson videos; to the head teacher at Farringdon School and Sports College, for allowing his outreach coordinator to be involved in the teaching of pupils involved in the production of the primary lesson videos; and to the head teacher and members of the Physical Education Department at The Minster School, Southwell, Nottinghamshire, for being involved in the production of the secondary lesson videos and for the use of the development plan in the case study materials. Thanks also to the head teacher of Shiremoor Primary School, North Tyneside, and the two physical education coordinators, for allowing the use of the physical education development plan in the case study materials; to the head teacher and deputy head teacher at Mayfield School, Hensingham, Cumbria, for allowing the use of materials illustrating the self-evaluation form (SEF) content; and to the head teacher and head of department at Biddick School and Sports College, for allowing the use of a SEF for Physical Education as part of case study material.

Finally, thanks to Merle Hunt, Howard Todd, Carole Raymond HMI, Clare Stretch and Glen Beaumont, for their review of the content of the material.

Key to Icons

	Quotes from other resources
	Quotes from the accompanying DVD
	Case study material from real schools
	Pre-course tasks for the taught course
	Mid-course tasks for the taught course
	Post-course tasks for the taught course
	Task

Abstract

Abbreviations

ACCAC	Qualifications Curriculum and Assessment Authority for Wales
AFD	Area(s) for development
AFI	Areas for improvement
afPE	Association for Physical Education
ALIS	Advanced Level Information System
ANO	Another
ANP	Another person
ANQ	Yet another person
AOTTs	Adults other than teachers
APEL	Accredited Prior Experiential Learning
APPG	All Party Parliamentary Group
AQA	Assessment and Qualifications Alliance
AST	Advanced skills teacher
baalpe	British Association of Advisers and Lecturers in Physical Education
BTEC	Business and Technology Education Council
CAT	Cognitive ability test
CB	Counterbalance
C of G	Centre of gravity
CPD	Continuing professional development
CRB	Criminal Records Bureau
CSLA	Community Sports Leaders' Award
D&T	Design and technology
DCMS	Department for Culture, Media and Sport
DDP	Department development plan
DfES	Department for Education and Skills
DIP	Department improvement plan
EAL	English as an additional language
ECM	Every Child Matters
EF	Evidence form
EiC	Excellence in Cities
EMG	Ethnic minority group
ENG	English
ESW	Education social worker
FFT	Fisher Family Trust (data)
FS	Foundation Stage
FSM	Free school meals

G&T	Gifted and Talented
H&S	Health and safety
HA	Higher attaining (pupils)
HEI	Higher education institute
HMI	Her Majesty's Inspectorate
HO	Higher order
HoD	Head of Department
HQPESS	High Quality Physical Education and School Sport
HRE	Health-related Exercise
ICT	Information and Communication Technology
IEP	Individual Education Plan
IIP	Investors in People
INSET	In-service educational training
IT	Information Technology
ITT	Initial Teacher Training
JAE	Junior Athlete Education
JSLA	Junior Sports Leaders' Award
K&U	Knowledge and understanding
KS	Key stage
LA	Lower attaining (pupils)
LDs	Learning difficulties
LEA	Local education authority
LOs	Learning outcomes
LPSA	Local Public Service Agreement
LSA	Learning support assistant
Ly/Ny	Literacy/numeracy
MA	Middle-attaining (pupils)
MAG	Minimum Acceptable Grade
MC	Mixed ability class
MFL	Modern foreign language
MIDYIS	Middle Years Information System
MLD	Moderate learning difficulties
National PESS PDP	National Physical Education and School Sport Professional Development Programme
NC	National Curriculum
NCPE	National Curriculum for Physical Education
NGB	National governing body
NOF3	New Opportunities Fund 3

NV+	Non-verbal
OAA	Outdoor and adventurous activities
OCR	Exam board
Ofsted	Office for Standards in Education
OIN	Ofsted identification number
OSHL	Out-of-school-hours learning
PANDA	Performance and Assessment Report
PE	Physical Education
PESS	Physical Education and School Sport
PLT	Primary link teacher
PM	Performance management
PP	PowerPoint
PTA	Parent Teachers' Association
QCA	Qualifications and Curriculum Authority
RPI	Relative performance indicator
SAQ	Speed, agility, quickness
SATs	Standard Attainment Tests
SE	Self-evaluation
SEF	Self-evaluation form
SEN	Special educational needs
SIG	School Improvement Grant
SIP	Subject improvement plan
SL	A class setted, streamed or banded by ability, where pupils are in the lower ability range within the school
SMT	Senior management team
SSCO	School Sport Coordinator
T	Teacher
T and L	Teaching and learning
TA	Teacher assessment
TA (on evidence form)	Teaching assistant
TJ	Triple jump
V+	Verbal (strong)
V-	Verbal (weak)
VAK	Visual, auditory, kinaesthetic
WB	Whiteboard
XC	Extra curricular
YELLIS	Year Eleven Information System

FOI Inspections: Evidence Form Codes

Observation Type
Required in all EFs

L   for lesson observations

A   for analysis of pupils' work

D   for discussions

O   for any other EFs.

Year Group(s)
Required in all EFs coded L and A

For single year groups use:

N   for **Nursery** classes

R   for **Reception** classes

1–13 for classes in **Y1–Y13**.

Grouping
Required only in EFs coded L

MC   **Mixed** ability class

SU   A class **Setted** or streamed or banded by ability where pupils are in the **Upper** ability range within the school

SA   A class **Setted** or streamed or banded by ability where pupils are in the **Average** ability range within the school

SL   A class **Setted** or streamed or banded by ability where pupils are in the **Lower** ability range within the school

O   **Other** forms of organisation.

BO   A **boys** only class

GI   A **girls** only class

MI   A **mixed gender** class

Present/number on Roll (NOR)
Required only in EFs coded L

Support Teachers and Assistants
Required only in EFs coded L

SEN   Teachers/assistants who support pupils with special educational needs

EAL   Teachers/assistants who support pupils with English as an additional language

OTH   Any other teachers/assistants who provide support

T   Support teachers

S   Assistants

Overview

Welcome to this self-evaluation workbook for leaders of physical education in primary, secondary and special schools, produced by the British Association of Advisers and Lecturers in Physical Education (baalpe) and the Association for Physical Education (afPE).

Overall Aim of the Training

The training aims to provide leaders of physical education in schools with the essential competencies to undertake rigorous self-evaluation of the work of the subject as part of the leadership and management of sustainable improvement.

What Will the Workbook Cover?

The workbook is designed to help leaders of physical education in primary, secondary and special schools develop the essential competencies of self-evaluation. Participants will therefore learn to monitor, evaluate, review and improve the work in their subject.

The training encourages the rigorous application of national criteria to case study material and participants' own settings, using:

- the expectations of Ofsted through the Common Inspection Framework, including 'Every Child Matters' (2005)

- the expectations of the DfES through the criteria set out for 'High Quality Physical Education and School Sport' (DfES, 2004).

The training focuses on applying the criteria to a wide range of evidence in order to evaluate:

- learners' standards and achievement

- the quality of provision, especially the teaching and learning

- the quality of leadership and management.

The training helps participants to:

- identify strengths and weaknesses in the work of the subject

- record their findings on a self-evaluation form

- make realistic plans for sustainable improvement.

Why Are These Essential Competencies Important?

The key leadership skills associated with self-evaluation and continuous improvement are increasingly important in the light of the government's development of its 'New Relationships with Schools', which shifts the responsibility for self-evaluation as the basis for improvement towards schools.

Ofsted believes that schools are best placed to recognise their own strengths and weaknesses in order to crucially do something about improving and developing them.

The 'lighter-touch', but no less rigorous, Ofsted inspections from September 2005 focus on checking the quality of a school's self-evaluation and its effectiveness in bringing about improvement.

The focus on high-quality teaching and learning is increasingly important under the revised arrangements for teacher appraisal and performance management.

The training will prepare teachers to meet the DfES/baalpe subject leader standards.

How Long Does the Training Last and What Tasks are Expected and Assessed?

The workbook can be used for self-study or as part of a taught course.

It will be essential to have a copy of baalpe's *A Guide to Self-review in Physical Education* (2006) in order to complete the course successfully.

You will need a copy of your own subject SEF and improvement/development/action plan.

The training takes participants through the process of self-evaluation using case study material and tasks, which require leaders to carry out self-evaluation activities in their own settings.

Taught Course

The course is designed to be taught over a period of around 10 weeks (eg over the course of one term). There will be two taught days. Participants are required to carry out pre-course, mid-course and post-course tasks based on their own workplace settings. These are identified throughout the workbook.

Self-study

For participants who wish to use this resource without attending the taught course, it is suggested that the identified tasks are undertaken with a mentor within the school, following the order in which they appear in the workbook.

School-based Research Tasks

The completion of school-based research tasks is essential in order to make progress. The tasks are designed to develop the essential skills, knowledge and understanding required to undertake self-evaluation and give the opportunity to practise and apply what has been learnt in participants' own settings.

Leaders working through this document independently will need to complete the tasks marked with the logo on the left, preferably in the order they occur, whether they are marked pre-course, mid-course or post course. Some participants undertaking self-study may not wish to undertake the optional tasks.

Leaders undertaking the taught course will complete tasks at the appropriate times during the training. These may be required during the taught days, pre-course, mid-course or post-course, as identified below.

- **Pre-course tasks**

  These are mandatory and essential preparation for the course.

  - Complete baalpe's *A Guide to Self-review in Physical Education* (2006).

  - Download a copy of the SEF for use in the training (some participants may wish to work electronically when on the course).

  - Collect all essential materials prior to the course (see Unit 1).

  - Complete Tasks 1, 2, 3 and 4 outlined in Unit 1, and Tasks 10, 11 and 14 of Unit 2.

- **Mid-course tasks**

  These make use of the material presented in Day 1 of the taught course and require further work within the context of participants' own schools.

  - Access the QCA website and download three case studies that you deem most relevant. Critique these and share them electronically with course participants prior to attendance on Day 2 (taught course).

  - Complete the following tasks:
    Unit 1 – Task 8
    Unit 2 – Tasks 16 and 17
    Unit 3 – Tasks 22, 23, 24, 25, 27 and 28
    Unit 4 – Tasks 29, 30 and 32.

- **Post-course tasks**

  - Complete Tasks 31 and 33 in Unit 4.

  - Complete the SEF fully (adapt and develop in light of the course if you have already completed it).

  - Complete a new department development plan (DDP)/department improvement plan (DIP).

  - Participants are to arrange their own e-learning network from the taught course and to share practice.

- **Training Day tasks**
  Unit 1 – Tasks 5, 6 and 7
  Unit 2 – Tasks 9, 12, 13 and 15
  Unit 3 – Tasks 18, 19, 20, 21 and 26
  Unit 4 – Task 34.

Differentiation

Some participants undertaking self-study may already have a good understanding of self-evaluation and school improvement, and may not wish to undertake the optional tasks.

Assessment

Participants wishing to be accredited will be required to attend the taught course and successfully complete all tasks. After completing the Self-evaluation Continuing Professional Development (SECPD) form, participants should use their professional development record to demonstrate the impact of their Self-evaluation professional development in the workplace. Participants may then wish to submit their portfolio of evidence for accredited prior experiential learning (APEL) towards a higher qualification at any higher education institute (HEI).

Case Study Materials

The two DVDs included in the pack provide filmed lessons in both primary and secondary schools.

The **primary case study material** is set in a primary school in Sunderland. The material on the DVD includes:

- a description of the school by the head teacher

- a description of a Year 2 class and lesson given by an advanced skills teacher (AST)/outreach coordinator

- a Year 2 lesson on basic skills taught by the advanced skills teacher (AST)/outreach coordinator

- evaluation and feedback of the lesson given by the class teacher to the AST/outreach coordinator

- a description of a Year 6 class and lesson given by the class teacher

- a Year 6 gymnastics lesson taught by the class teacher

- evaluation and feedback of the lesson given by the AST/outreach coordinator to the class teacher.

The **secondary case study material** is set in a secondary community school in Nottinghamshire. The material on the DVD includes:

- a description of the school by the head teacher

- a description of a Year 7 class and lesson, which is led by the head of physical education (PE)

- a Year 7 athletics lesson taught by the head of PE

- evaluation and feedback of the lesson given by the AST to the head of PE

- a description of a Year 10 class and lesson, which is given by the AST

- a Year 10 GCSE theory lesson taught by the AST

- evaluation and feedback of the lesson given by the head of PE to the AST.

Scripts of this material can be found in Appendix I (Primary) and Appendix II (Secondary). Where quotations from these scripts are used in the resource, you will find this icon.

Appendix III (a completed secondary school SEF for PE) is also used.

Other case study material, including contributions from a special school, is placed at appropriate points within the units or in the appendices. These are identified by the symbol on the left.

Throughout the training, reference is made to essential documents, useful websites and support materials.

Link Between the Action Research Model and the Self-evaluation Course

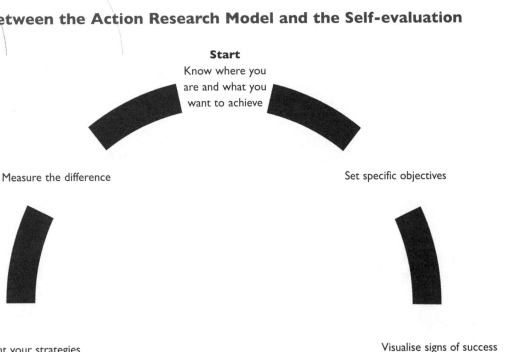

Start
Know where you are and what you want to achieve

Measure the difference

Set specific objectives

Implement your strategies

Visualise signs of success

Take a baseline

Identify strategies that will work

Figure 1: The Action Research Model – National PESS Professional Development Programme

The Action Research model outlined in Figure 1 underpins schools' improvement planning as developed through participation in the National PESS PDP.

This training (Self-evaluation in Physical Education) builds on the knowledge, skills and understanding of self-evaluation activities and school improvement planning that participants may already have developed through the National PESS PDP.

The self-evaluation activities developed in Units 1, 2 and 3 are the equivalent of the first step in the cycle – 'knowing where you are and what you want to achieve'. Unit 4 focuses on key leadership skills, especially planning for improvement.

By the end of the self-evaluation training, participants will have sufficient experience to carry out self-evaluation activities that support the Action Research model outlined above. They will be more confident about making accurate evaluations and identifying areas for improvement.

National Expectations and Criteria

Criteria for DfES High-quality Physical Education and School Sport

In 2003, the Department for Education and Skills (DfES) and the Department for Culture, Media and Sport (DCMS) set out the National School Sport Strategy.

The strategy's aim is to deliver the government's target to '…increase the percentage of school children who spend a minimum of two hours each week on high-quality PE and school sport within and beyond the curriculum from 25% in 2002 to 75% in 2006…to 85% by 2008'. (Announced December 2004.)

The National School Sport Strategy – High-quality Outcomes

Young people:

1. are **committed**. They:

   • seldom miss PE lessons or opportunities to take part in school sport

   • get changed and ready for lessons on time

   • are available for school matches, festivals and performances

   • take responsibility for not letting down others in school

   • encourage others to get involved

   • help adults to organise and manage lessons and sports activities.

2. **know and understand** what they are trying to achieve. They:

   • know the difference between how they have to think for each area of activity in the National Curriculum for Physical Education (NCPE)

   • know when and how to use the principles of composition, choreography, games strategy, athletics tactics and problem solving

   • are clear about how they are going to be judged in each area of activity.

3. understand that PE and sport form part of a **healthy, active lifestyle**. They:

   • know how their participation in PESS contributes to a balanced healthy, active lifestyle

   • can describe how each activity they get involved in affects their fitness, health and feelings about themselves

   • are able to explain how the school helps them to maintain a healthy, active lifestyle.

4. have the **confidence** to get involved in PE and sport. They:

   • are willing to demonstrate what they can do, and volunteer questions and answers

   • ask for help when they need it and take the initiative to help others

   • are keen to take part in a range of PESS opportunities, including clubs and examination courses

   • are ready to take part as a player, leader, coach, administrator or spectator

   • talk positively about what they have achieved

   • are willing to try new ideas, roles and activities without worrying about failing.

5. have the **skill and control** that they need to take part in PE and sport. They:

   • show good body control and movement

   • have poise and balance

   • have a wide range of skills and techniques that they can apply and adapt effectively

   • show good fluency and accuracy in their movements.

6. **willingly take part in** a range of competitive, creative and challenge-type activities. They:

   • are always happy to get involved in any activities on offer

   • choose to get involved in more than one type of activity

   • are content to work and perform on their own, as well as in groups and teams.

7. **think about and make appropriate decisions** for themselves. They:

   • work without constant prompting and direction from the teacher

   • ask questions that help them to organise themselves and make progress

   • come up with and explain a wide range of ideas and strategies to help them improve

   • vary and adapt what they do, taking into account others' strengths and weaknesses

   • react to situations intelligently when performing.

8. show **a desire to improve and achieve** in relation to their own abilities. They:

   • show determination to achieve best results

   • spend extra time practising and training

   • often compare their performance to their own in the past and to other people's

   • often feel that their work or performance could be better still

   • ask for advice and information on how to improve their attainment and the quality of their performance.

9. have the **stamina**, **suppleness and strength** to keep going. They:

   • have high levels of concentration

   • maintain their activity and energy levels

   • seldom miss PE because of illness or injury

   • are physically strong and flexible enough to take part in activities in lessons.

10. **enjoy** PE, school and community sport. They:

   • are keen to take part in what is going on

   • talk about what they are doing with enthusiasm

   • show an interest in the PESS notice boards

   • make time to take part in PESS, and often watch or read about PESS

   • are eager to get to PE lessons

   • smile often.

See the DfES publication 'High Quality PE and Sport for Young people – A Guide to Recognising and Achieving High Quality PE and Sport in Schools and Clubs'.

Ofsted – 'Every Child Matters – Framework for the inspection of schools in England from September 2005'

From September 2005, the common inspection framework asked schools to evaluate:

• achievement and standards

1. How well do learners achieve? Schools must evaluate:
    - the standards learners reach as indicated by their test and examination results; any significant variations between groups of learners, subjects, courses and key stages; trends over time; comparisons with other schools; whether learners reach challenging targets

    - the standards of current work in relation to their learning goals (noting any significant differences between current work and recent results)

    - learners' progress relative to their starting points and capabilities, with any significant variations between groups of learners, making clear whether there are any groups underachieving.

1a. How good is the overall personal development and well-being of learners? Schools must evaluate:
    - behaviour; attendance; emotional development

    - spiritual, moral, social and cultural development.

'Every Child Matters' (ECM) Criteria

1. The extent to which providers enable learners to **be healthy**:
    - All learners, including those with learning difficulties and disabilities, undertake PE and school sport for at least two hours per week.

    - Learners are discouraged from smoking and substance abuse and supported in giving up. Learners are educated about sexual risks.

    - Learners are encouraged and enabled to eat healthily.

    - Learners are encouraged to drink water at regular intervals.

    - Learners are taught to recognise signs of personal stress and develop strategies to manage it.

    - Staff are advised and supported in identifying possible physical and mental health problems and making appropriate referrals.

    - Learners have access to an appropriate range of support if they feel troubled.

2. The extent to which providers ensure that learners **stay safe**:
    - Disaster plans are in place.

    - Learners are taught to swim in accordance with the National Curriculum.

    - Staff are trained to identify risks and manage them.

    - CRB and other vetting checks are undertaken for staff either working with learners or having regular unsupervised contact with them. These are regularly updated.

    - The provider has designated/named members of staff for child protection, who receive regular training.

    - Staff with responsibility for child protection work are supported and supervised commensurate with their roles.

- Threshold criteria for making and responding to child protection referrals are clear and widely understood.

3. How well learners **enjoy and achieve**:
   - Support is given to learners with poor behaviour and attendance.
   - The provider monitors learners' personal and academic development and plans provision to reflect this.
   - The provider's development planning targets the needs of potentially underachieving learners.

4. The extent to which learners **make a positive contribution**:
   - Learners understand their rights and responsibilities.
   - Learners feel free from bullying and discrimination.
   - Learners initiate and manage a range of organised activities within the provider's – and, for older learners, community – organisation(s).
   - Learners, individually and collectively, are consulted and their views are listened to when key decisions affecting them have to be made.
   - Maintained secondary schools implement a programme of education that gives learners the knowledge and understanding to become informed and responsible citizens.
   - Effective action is taken to reduce bullying and discrimination by learners.
   - The provider has clear policies on combating bullying and discrimination by learners.
   - Learners who are victims of bullying or harassment are advised how to raise their concerns and are given good access to support.

5. The extent to which providers enable learners to **achieve economic well-being**:
   - Learners are supported in developing self-confidence, team-working skills and enterprising qualities.
   - Impartial careers advice is available for all 14–19-year-olds and personal support is given as needed.
   - Work-based learning is available for all learners in Key Stage 4.
   - All Key Stage 4 learners undertake work-related learning and useful work experience.
   - The provider takes steps to ensure that learners are financially literate.

• the quality of provision

2. How effective are teaching, training and learning? Schools must evaluate:
   - how well teaching and resources promote learning, address the full range of learners' needs and meet course programme requirements
   - the suitability and rigour of assessment in planning and monitoring learners' progress
   - the identification of, and provision for, additional learning needs
   - where appropriate, the involvement of parents and carers in their children's learning and development.

3. How well do the curriculum programmes and activities meet the needs and interests of learners? Schools must evaluate:
   - the extent to which programmes match learners' aspirations and potential, building on prior attainment and experience

- how far programmes meet external requirements and are responsive to local circumstances

- the extent to which employers' needs are met

- the extent to which enrichment activities and/or extended services contribute to learner enjoyment

- the extent to which the provision contributes to the learners' capacity to stay safe and healthy.

4. How well are learners guided and supported? Schools must evaluate:

- the care, advice, guidance and other support provided to safeguard welfare, promote personal development and achieve high standards

- the quality and accessibility of information, advice and guidance for learners in relation to courses and programmes and, where applicable, career progression.

• leadership and management

5. How effective are leadership and management in raising achievement and supporting all learners? Schools must evaluate:

- how effectively performance is monitored and improved through quality assurance and self-assessment

- how effectively leaders and managers at all levels clearly direct improvement and promote the well-being of learners through high-quality care, education and training

- how well equality of opportunity is promoted and discrimination tackled so that all learners achieve their potential

- the adequacy and suitability of specialist equipment, learning resources and accommodation

- how effectively and efficiently resources are deployed to achieve value for money

- how effectively links are made with other providers, services, employers and other organisations to promote the integration of care, education and any extended services to enhance learning and to promote well-being

- the effectiveness with which governors and other supervisory boards discharge their responsibilities.

• the school's overall effectiveness

6. What is the overall effectiveness of the provision, including any extended services and its main strengths and weaknesses?

- How effective and efficient are the provision and related services in meeting the full range of learners' needs and why?

- What is the capacity to make improvements?

- How effective have any steps taken to promote improvement since the last inspection been?

- Quality and standards in the Foundation Stage.

- The effectiveness and efficiency of the sixth form.

See the Ofsted website for the most up-to-date versions: www.ofsted.gov.uk
'Every Child Matters – Framework for the Inspection of Schools in England from September 2005'. (Ofsted, 2005).

Unit 1: Introduction to Self-evaluation

Purpose and Aims

Unit 1 sets out to establish what is meant by self-evaluation, and its importance as a means of raising standards and improving experiences of physical education and school sport for every learner.

The tasks and activities help participants to analyse and understand the expectations set out for high-quality physical education and school sport by the DfES, and to understand how these relate to the Ofsted criteria for effectiveness, taking account of 'Every Child Matters'.

The Ofsted Self-evaluation Form (SEF) is used as a basis for the judgements that need to be made. In this unit, the process of self-evaluation and its link to development and improvement are explored. The sources of evidence needed to make the judgements are considered. The skills needed to evaluate the evidence are practised.

From the outset, this session makes clear that self-evaluation is only worthwhile if it leads to action for improvement.

Unit 1 Learning Outcomes

By the end of this unit, participants will:

- understand the purpose of self-evaluation and its underlying principles
- recognise the links between high-quality physical education and school sport, and Ofsted criteria for effective schools (including 'Every Child Matters')
- be aware of the key sources of evidence needed for effective self-evaluation
- be aware of the need to plan for manageable self-evaluation and improvement.

Requirements

You will need:

- 'Every Child Matters – Framework for the inspection of schools in England from September 2005'. (Ofsted, 2005) Ref: HMI 2435
- 'Guidance for Inspectors of Schools: Using the Evaluation Schedule'. (Ofsted, 2005) Ref: HMI 2504
- 'Guidance for the Inspection of Schools: Conducting the Inspection'. (Ofsted, 2005) Ref: HMI 2502
- a School Self-evaluation Form (SEF) – available from the Ofsted website, www.ofsted.gov.uk
- 'High Quality Physical Education and School Sport' (DfES, 2004)
- *A Guide to Self-review in Physical Education* (baalpe, 2006)
- *Achieving Excellence* (baalpe, 2004).

Unit Development

1.1 Why Self-evaluate?

1.2 What is Self-evaluation?

1.3 Principles of Effective Self-evaluation

1.4 The Self-evaluation Form (SEF)

1.5 Aiming to be At Least Good – Recognising the relationship between the expectations of Ofsted for effective schools, including 'Every Child Matters', and the DfES expectations for 'High Quality Physical Education and School Sport'

1.6 Collecting and Analysing Key Sources of Evidence

1.7 Keeping an Overview of Findings from Self-evaluation Activity and Building a Manageable Plan of Self-evaluation Activity.

Table 1: Summary of tasks for Unit 1

	Pre-course Task 1 (3 hours)	Work on your own or with a colleague and complete the tasks in baalpe's *A Guide to Self-review in Physical Education*.
	Pre-course Task 2 (30 minutes)	What does self-evaluation mean to you? Compile a list of examples of self-evaluation activity used in your school. What is being evaluated? Who is being informed? Have they led to improvement?
	Pre-course Task 3 (30 minutes)	From your own experience, what do you consider are the underlying principles of effective self-evaluation? What will make it work?
	Pre-course Task 4 (30 minutes) Optional Task	List as many methods of collecting key sources of evidence as you can think of.
	Task 5 (30 minutes) Optional Task	You have already identified evaluation activities undertaken in your school (see Pre-course Task 2). Consider each of the 11 principles provided in the task and indicate whether they underpin self-evaluation activity in your school. Highlight those that were evident. Indicate the principles that do and do not underpin self-evaluation activity in your school. State the reasons for this and identify what could be done to ensure that the principle in question is followed.
	Task 6 (30 minutes) Optional Task	Analyse and evaluate sections of sample SEFs or use your own school's SEF.
	Task 7 (20 minutes)	Make links between the Ofsted 'Every Child Matters' framework and criteria and the DfES expectations for 'High Quality Physical Education and School Sport'.
	Task 8 (30 minutes) (Ongoing throughout each unit)	Keep an overview of issues arising from self-evaluation activities and build a manageable plan of self-evaluation activities.

Pre-course Task 1 (3 hours)

Work on your own or with a colleague and complete the tasks in baalpe's *A Guide to Self-review in Physical Education.*

Pre-course Task 2 (30 minutes)

What does self-evaluation mean to you?

Work on your own or with a colleague and compile a list of examples of activities that contribute to self-evaluation that are already used in your school.

- What is being evaluated?

- Who is being informed?

- In what way have they led to improvement?

Self-evaluation activity	What does it evaluate?	Who does it inform?
1.		
2.		
3.		
4.		
How have the activities led to improvement?		
1.		
2.		
3.		
4.		

Pre-course Task 3 (30 minutes)

From your own experience, what do you consider are the underlying principles of effective self-evaluation? What will make it work? Work on your own or preferably with a colleague(s).

The underlying principles of self-evaluation:
What will make it work:

Pre-course Task 4 (30 minutes) – Optional Task

Work on your own or preferably with a colleague(s).

- List as many methods of collecting key sources of evidence as you can think of.
- Tick those that you already collect. Put a star against those you do not.
- Tick the areas of the framework for which the source provides evidence.

Key sources of evidence for self-evaluation	Tick if you already gather this evidence and star if you do not	Standards and achievement	Personal development	Teaching and assessment	Curriculum	Care	Leadership and management

1.1 Why Self-evaluate?

Effective self-evaluation is recognised as the key to school improvement and raising standards in schools.

Rigorous self-evaluation helps schools to improve; it should not be undertaken solely for the purpose of inspection…To offer the best possible education for learners, staff and governors should know how well their school provides for them, the impact of this provision and how it can be improved. Thorough self-evaluation provides the best means to identify strengths and weaknesses: from these, arise the key priorities for improvement.

DfES 'A New Relationship with Schools: Improving Performance through Self-evaluation', 2004.

The main reason to carry out self-evaluation of the quality of Physical Education and School Sport (PESS) in your school is to collect information that you can use to:

- increase the number of pupils showing most of the characteristics of the outcomes of high-quality PESS

- improve the quality of PESS provision to ensure that more pupils demonstrate the outcomes.

'The Impact of Self-evaluation on Pupils' Achievement
of High Quality Outcomes in PE and School Sport', QCA, 2004.

Quote from a secondary head teacher:

PE in 1995 was declared to be an unsatisfactory department…We've needed to make sure that there has been a good robust journey of improvement….Now it is an outstanding department…it has been achieved by a really good focus on high-quality teaching and learning. In 2000, the whole school was judged to be underachieving. It was really useful to us because what it made us do was really focus upon school self-evaluation and continuous improvement across the school and, in many ways, the success that PE had enjoyed earlier to move things on in terms of standards and quality of provision gave us the model from which to develop our whole school approaches.

Phil Blinston, Head Teacher, The Minster School, Southwell, Nottinghamshire
(For the full interview, see the DVD under Secondary Case Study Material – Description of the School).

Quote from a primary head teacher:

We generally do self-evaluation through auditing. Recently, the sports co-ordinator, PE coordinator met and did an audit for the staff…There were areas of the curriculum we weren't very sure about so we consulted Farringdon (Community Sports College) and their outreach coordinator, Jill Sheridan, came down and she has supplemented those areas which we think were weakened. We were not so good at gymnastics and we're not so good in dance…and Jill has been able to come on a weekly basis and help us enormously in the learning.

Geoff Bolton, Head Teacher, East Herrington Primary School, Sunderland
(For the full interview, see the DVD under Primary Case Study Material – Description of the School).

In the annual Ofsted physical education reports, HMI identified evaluation as an area for improvement in physical education in leadership and management in both primary and secondary schools.

Primary

Main findings…Leadership and management are satisfactory or better in the great majority of schools. However, as in previous years, aspects of monitoring and evaluating the subject remain significant areas for improvement.

'The Annual Report of Her Majesty's Chief Inspector of Schools 2004/05. Physical Education in Primary Schools', Ofsted, October 2005.

Secondary

Main findings…Although leadership and management are generally good, evaluation remains an area of weakness.

'The Annual Report of Her Majesty's Chief Inspector of Schools 2004/05. Physical Education in Secondary Schools', Ofsted, October 2005.

1.2 What is Self-evaluation?

Self-evaluation means asking basic questions:

- How well are we doing? (ie evaluation of evidence gathered through monitoring activities against clear criteria.)
- How do we know? (ie analysis of the evidence gathered.)
- What do we need to improve? (ie identification of what needs to be improved.)

These are the basis of the questions posed in the school self-evaluation form (SEF).

These basic questions are asked of:

- the major outcomes for a school/subject – the standards, achievement and personal development of learners
- the effectiveness of provision on the outcomes for learners – especially teaching and learning
- the effectiveness of leadership and management on outcomes and improvement.

1.3 Principles of Effective Self-evaluation

What factors are likely to make self-evaluation work and lead to school improvement? To be effective, the self-evaluation process should:

- be simple, not burdensome, and integrate with a school's routine management systems (ie a common framework)
- have consistent expectations based on national expectation
- include supported self-analysis based on openness, honesty and trust, and involve clear communication
- involve staff, learners, parents and governors at all levels
- ask the most important questions about learners' learning, achievements and development

- be inclusive, considering the achievement of all learners
- use a telling range of evidence to answer the questions
- benchmark the school's and learners' performance against the best comparable schools
- listen to, and do something about, the views of the major stakeholders (ie the learners and parents)
- be about sharing best practice as well as identifying areas for improvement
- lead to action and improvement.

Task 5 (30 minutes) – Optional Task

You have already identified evaluation activities undertaken in your school (see Pre-course Task 2).

Consider each of the 11 principles below and indicate whether they underpin self-evaluation activity in your school. Highlight principles that were evident.

Indicate in the box below, the principles that **do** and **do not** underpin self-evaluation activity in your school. State the reasons for this and identify what could be done to ensure that the principle in question is followed.

Work on your own or preferably with a colleague(s).

Principles that should underpin self-evaluation activity in your school Principles that:	Tick or cross, and state the reasons why the principle does or does not underpin self-evaluation in your own setting. if it does not, what can be done to ensure that the principle is followed?
1. are simple, not burdensome, and integrate with a school's routine management systems (ie a common framework)	
2. have consistent expectations based on national expectation	
3. include supported self-analysis based on openness, honesty and trust, and involve clear communication	
4. involve staff, learners, parents and governors at all levels	
5. ask the most important questions about learners' learning, achievements and development	

6. are inclusive, considering the achievement of all learners	
7. use a telling range of evidence to answer the questions	
8. benchmark the school's and learners' performance against the best comparable schools	
9. listen to, and do something about, the views of the major stakeholders (ie the learners and parents)	
10. are about sharing best practice as well as identifying areas for improvement	
11. lead to action and improvement	

1.4 The Self-evaluation Form (SEF)

The Self-evaluation Form (SEF) was introduced by Ofsted as a means of helping schools carry out their own self-evaluation. The SEF requires schools to make judgements about the outcomes for a school and the effectiveness of its provision using the headings of the Ofsted Framework. It should be an **accurate diagnostic document** with **all conclusions fully supported by evidence**. It should indicate the key strengths and weaknesses and what needs to be tackled to bring about improvement.

Though not a legal requirement, it is recommended that schools keep the SEF up to date at least annually.

The SEF records school's self-evaluation but does not prescribe the process. The SEF is a **summary of the self-evaluation activities**. It will be for schools to develop **their own process** of self-evaluation to contribute to the SEF and to fit the completion of the SEF into their core systems as best suits them.

School leaders are encouraged to use the SEF as a vehicle for dialogue with middle managers. Senior leaders in schools are encouraging subject leaders to use the SEF as a guide to self-evaluation activity and improvement planning. Subject SEFs then usefully inform the school SEF and improvement planning.

Appendix III contains a SEF completed by the leader of physical education and sport in a sports college.

You will find this a useful document to refer to throughout the course.

The SEF helps schools and subject leaders to:
- analyse the evidence they have gathered rigorously
- demonstrate clear judgements based on secure evidence
- identify key priorities in order to plan the action needed to bring about change.

Order of Completion of a SEF

1. The sections on **achievement and standards and personal development and well-being should be completed first** since these outcomes will form the basis of your judgements in other sections.

2. The sections relating to provision are completed next: **teaching and learning, curriculum and other activities, care, guidance and support**, making sure that their impact on learner outcomes is at the heart of the evaluations.

3. The section on the **effectiveness and efficiency of leadership and management**, ensuring that account is taken of the impact of leadership and management activities on improving standards and the quality of provision, is completed next.

4. Finally, you are ready to complete the section on **overall effectiveness**.

In order to make the overall judgements in each section, make use of the criteria outlined in *A Guide to Self-review in Physical Education* (baalpe, 2006), which is used as part of Pre-course Task 1 and set out in each relevant section. **Refer to Pre-course Task 1.**

1.4.1 Analysis of Sections of Exemplar SEFs

What is written in the SEF is a summary of your evaluation of the evidence gathered. It should intelligently analyse the evidence by identifying strengths, weaknesses and priorities for improvement.

Criteria for a Good SEF

Your SEF should:
- convey a clear picture of how well the subject/school is doing
- provide proof of how you know what you know
- show what you are doing to build on successes and remedy weaknesses.

Look for:
- clear judgements based on the framework criteria
- judgements that are supported by a good range of key evidence
- strengths, weaknesses and priorities for improvement that are clearly identified
- links between issues raised in the achievement section and how the school is tackling these in the sections on provision and leadership and management.

Case Study Examples of Summaries of Evidence

Consider the merits of the examples from various schools set out below. (The names of the schools have been omitted.)

Primary School

4. Personal Development and Well-being

4a. To What Extent Do Learners Adopt Healthy Lifestyles?

This is an area of school development that has shown huge improvement since the last inspection. Health education is a focus from nursery, where children have grown and eaten their own food, through to Year 6, where children are involved in a huge range of activities.

The following bullet points illustrate the breadth of achievements at the school:

- Active Mark 2004
- Healthy School Award
- science curriculum
- lunchtime fitness club (KS 1) – 90 children take part
- lunchtime skipping club (KS 1) – 90 children take part
- after-school dance club (KS 2 with visiting coach) – 30 children take part
- netball club (KS 2) – 28 children involved (league winners second year running)
- tennis club (KS 2) – 20 children, mixed (area champions)
- judo club (KS 2 with visiting coach) – 40 children, mixed
- jump rope (British Heart Foundation-sponsored event) – 33 children involved
- rounders club (KS 2) – 60 children involved
- termly 'walk to school' – whole-school initiative
- newly installed chilled water cooler available to all classes as a result of school-council intervention
- weekly swimming (KS 2) – 130 children involved
- a smoke-free school promoting substance-abuse awareness sessions through the science curriculum and external LEA input (Lucy's Bag KS 1)

At the school, we believe in a holistic approach to education and we are keen to emphasise that children develop both physically and spiritually. Consequently, the religious education (RE) programme is equally important in developing all-round health. Many children are encouraged to extend their physical activities at home, where many are members of local swimming, football, judo, dance, rugby, tennis clubs etc. Children are also encouraged to take part in our 'activity targets', where the focus is to achieve a set number of hours of physical activity outside the school day.

Healthy Week is an annual event organised by the school. It involves a wide range of activities, which benefit from the expertise of active, confident and enthusiastic staff, parents, professionals and LEA sports coordinators. Events during Healthy Week have included parent and child aerobics sessions, local walks and NHS parent visitors to talk about dental care, blood pressure and healthy food choices. During the Week, the science curriculum promotes healthy eating by encouraging all classes to produce their own healthy snacks, which have included fruit kebabs, healthy sandwiches, sugar-free jelly and fruit-juice lollies. The LEA has been so impressed with our efforts that we were selected to take part in a TV programme promoting healthy lifestyles.

Additionally, the school tries to encourage healthy eating through a wide selection of healthy options provided by the school meals service and by encouraging healthy choices with regard to the snacks provided by parents for break time. The school also supports the national Fruit for Schools scheme and children in KS 1 and Foundation Stage are encouraged to take fruit to school on a daily basis.

Special School – Part of a School Sport Partnership

Standards and Achievement

Where we are:
One hundred pupils are engaged in sports leadership, with 33% of young leaders actively employed in supporting out-of-school-hours learning (OSHL) in primary schools and 100% at festivals during curriculum time. Home-to-school transport limits the support leaders can commit off their own school site (as this is a rural area). There has been limited access for KS 4 and post-16 students to access national governing body (NGB) qualifications.

Where we want to get to:
Deploy more sports leaders to assist with activities outside the curriculum. More sports leaders accessing NGB courses.

Personal Development and Well-being

Where we are:

1. 23% of KS 1 pupils take part in at least one OSHL activity per week. The majority of these are in Year 2 but there is a good mix of girls and boys taking part.

2. 12% of KS 3 and 4 pupils participate regularly in OSHL. The current provision is limited by staff availability, facility availability and home-to-school transport.

3. The average percentage of children taking part in high-quality performance competition across the partnership is 37%. This is broken down as: KS 1 – 37%; KS 2 – 36%; KS 3 – 39% and KS 4 – 30%. Financial implications for transport and staffing issues tend to be barriers for some schools to provide more access to opportunities.

4. Pockets of KS 3 and KS 4 pupils have a low level of commitment to PESS, which is seen through lack of attendance, no kit and poor attitudes.

Where we want to get to:

1. More KS 1 pupils participating in OSHL activity each week. A higher number improving their skills and having the confidence to get involved in PESS.

2. More KS 3 and 4 pupils participating in OSHL activity each week. Young people willingly taking part in a range of competitive, creative and challenge-type activities.

3. More pupils from across the partnership taking part in inter-school opportunities. Multi-skill at KS 1 and multi-sport at KS 2 and 3.

4. The targeted groups enjoy PE and sport, are committed to PESS, have the confidence to get involved in PESS and show a desire to improve in relation to their own abilities.

Secondary School

Standards and Achievement in Key Stage 3

How are we doing?/How well should we be doing?

Transfer data is limited. On entry to Year 7, I (HoD) surveyed the gymnastic experience of the new Year 7 students. Less than 10% had real experience of gymnastics. The experiences of students from feeder schools are tremendously varied in other areas of the National Curriculum. Discussion with senior leaders in the summer term has established that the system for target setting for PE at intake, based on their academic prior attainment and capability, is inappropriate. An improved system in Y 7 will allow the department to set more accurate targets from now on. (The high prediction is just ridiculous, unrealistic!) That said, the KS 3 results for this year have been our best ever, and I am 99.9% confident that comparisons with national data, particularly the number achieving L6+, will be very good. The provision at feeder schools is comparable with the situation nationwide. The results this year, therefore, are a remarkable achievement, given the background experience of the intake students and the less-than-remarkable provision (accommodation) compared to many schools.

Standards and Achievement in Key Stage 4

How are we doing?/How well should we be doing?

Last year's Year 11 – not as well as we wanted, but not unexpected. Some students' papers have gone for re-marking. This may improve the results. This was an unusual cohort and the dip is by no means the start of a trend. The current Y 11 are doing well and the Y 10 have made a super start. Due to timetabling, classes are taught as single sex and at different times. I observed the groups formally and informally. This revealed some theory groups where attitudes were less than good. The girls' groups' lessons were always excellent (taught by an AST) but some pupils' attitudes were less than satisfactory. We were not able to implement our A/B and our C/D borderline strategies (due to timetabling). These have been successful in the past. For the current Y 11 and 10, timetabling means they all come down together. This allows the flexibility found elsewhere in the construction of groups and the range of practical activities on offer. This year, the practical arrangements have been the best ever. Last year's Y 11 had to cover all practical activities even if not relevant to their marks. For Y 11 and 10, this is not the case and will impact significantly on practical marks. This is one of the reasons students following the games route do so much better than the PE route.

Teaching and Learning

Twenty two lessons observed over a one-year period. Seventy-seven percent good or better, 14% satisfactory, 9% unsatisfactory.

Strengths

- Department team approach, commitment and willingness to pursue vision.

- Improved use of schemes of work and more thoughtful lesson preparation.

- Some extremely adept at sharing of lesson objectives and continual reference to, and assessment in terms of, learning outcomes.

- Excellence in teaching in some quarters.

- Effective teaching and learning with SEN and less practically able students.

Areas for Development

- Lesson planning – need for differentiated objectives clearly stated in planning for all key stages.

- Improving the quality of sharing of lesson objectives with students – clarity – and, whenever possible, increasing the time allocated for this (KS 4 and 5 – less easy outside on a cold wet day).

- Plenary – sometimes rushed, as at the end of a lesson, the collection of equipment and putting away of apparatus can hit a snag, eg discussion missing. Need to a) revisit the importance of the plenary and b) explore developing a plenary of greater length at the end of a learning episode (which might cover several lessons).

- Continue working on the strategies for extending the more able in all the key stages.

Task 6 (30 minutes) – Optional Task

Analyse and evaluate sections of an example SEF's or use your own school's SEF.

Working on your own or with a colleague(s), choose one example of a SEF and use the criteria for a good SEF to identify its strengths and weaknesses.

How well does the SEF/self-review help to answer the following questions?

- How well are we doing?
- How do we know?
- What do we need to improve?

Focusing on learners' achievement and personal development and well-being, fill in the boxes below.

How well does the SEF or your review help to answer the question, 'How well are we doing'?   What analysis is there of learners' achievement and personal development?

How well does the SEF or your review help to answer the question, 'How do we know'?   What evidence is used to base the judgements about achievement and personal development on?

How well does the SEF or your review help to answer the question, 'What do we need to improve'?   Does the SEF identify clear areas for improvement?

Critical Analysis of the Case Study Examples of Summaries of Evidence

Analysis of the SEF from Primary School – Personal Development and Well-being
How well does the SEF or your review help to answer the question, 'How well are we doing'? What analysis is there of learners' achievement and personal development? *This section gives a great deal of information about the school's provision and less about how the provision is affecting pupils' outcomes.* *How does the school know what impact this provision is having on pupils' health, physical development, enjoyment, social skills and self-confidence?*
How well does the SEF or your review help to answer the question, 'How do we know'? What evidence is used to base the judgements about achievement and personal development on? *The evidence provided is mostly about provision. Though the numbers of pupils taking part in extra-curricular activities are given, there is no indication as to how participation is affecting their achievement and enjoyment.*
How well does the SEF or your review help to answer the question, 'What do we need to improve'? Does the SEF identify clear areas for improvement? *No indication in this section of the SEF and/or what needs to be improved.*

Analysis of the SEF from Special School – Standards and Achievement, Personal Development and Well-being

How well does the SEF or your review help to answer the question, 'How well are we doing'?

What analysis is there of learners' achievement and personal development?

There is detail of the numbers/percentage of pupils involved in activities but not a great deal about the number achieving awards or NC levels. No judgements are given.

How well does the SEF or your review help to answer the question, 'How do we know'?

What evidence is used to base the judgements about achievement and personal development on?

The evidence is based on numbers/percentages taking part in activities.
Little evidence on what pupils actually achieve (ie how many gain the Sports Leader Award).

How well does the SEF or your review help to answer the question, 'What do we need to improve'?

Does the SEF identify clear areas for improvement?

This is set out in general terms but could be more specific and related to the NCPE.

Analysis of the SEF from Secondary School – Standard and Achievements, Teaching and Learning

How well does the SEF or your review help to answer the question, 'How well are we doing'?

What analysis is there of learners' standards and achievement?

The judgement made is that achievement in KS 3 is remarkable. Could give more detail about levels and progress from year to year to justify this judgement.
The judgement on KS 4 is not so clear. Are standards satisfactory, good or what?
It could be clearer where the excellent teaching is and what makes it excellent.

How well does the SEF or your review help to answer the question 'How do we know'?

What evidence is used to base the judgements about standards, achievement, teaching and learning on?

A good number of lessons have been observed by the leader of PE.

How well does the SEF or your review help to answer the question, 'What do we need to improve'?

Does the SEF identify clear areas for improvement?

Clear identification of areas for development in teaching and learning, but these are not indicated so clearly for standards and achievement.

Analysis of the SEF from Secondary School – Appendix III

How well does the SEF or your review help to answer the question, 'How well are we doing'?

What analysis is there of learners' standards and achievement?

There is little to give an overview of the nature of the pupils and which particular groups of pupils it will be worthwhile tracking through the SEF, to ensure that they are well supported and achieve.

A good outline section on identifying and analysing stakeholders' views.

Though good overall in reporting on standards, in that there is a summary of results for GCSE and KS 3 and KS 4 NC, this could be more detailed (eg there is no reference to the success of HA pupils/A*/A at GCSE).

There is little evaluation of the progress and achievement of learners overall or for groups of learners. There is little justification for the overall judgement of good standards and achievement other than the overall good results.

The layout of the section is helpful.

CM is well covered.

How well does the SEF or your review help to answer the question, 'How do we know'?

Specific and measurable targets for GCSE are given for MA and HA learners, but targets for NC are not clear and do not appear to take into account changes in KS 2 levels of prior attainment.

How well does the SEF or your review help to answer the question, 'What do we need to improve'?

Does the SEF identify clear areas for improvement?

Not all weaknesses in T and L section are tackled in the future targets section.

Overall, the SEF provides a useful overview of the work for the subject, identifying strengths well and areas for improvement. The AFI do not always become priorities for action.

1.5 Aiming to be At Least Good – Recognising the relationship between the expectations of Ofsted for effective schools, including 'Every Child Matters' and the DfES expectations for 'High Quality Physical Education and School Sport'

Task 7 (20 minutes)

Make links between the DfES outcomes of high-quality physical education and school sport and the Ofsted 'Every Child Matters' framework and criteria on which the self-evaluation form is based.

Refer to baalpe's *A Guide to Self-review in Physical Education* (2006) for the grade criteria for 'good' for each of the sections.

Identify three strengths in PE and school sport in your school, under each of the major Ofsted framework headings below.

Use the criteria for DfES High-quality Physical Education and School Sport (HQPESS) outlined on pages 10 and 11 and highlight the criteria that matches the strengths identified. Use baalpe's *A Guide to Self-review in Physical Education* to establish where there is plenty of evidence and where there is too little evidence and a need to find out more.

Work on your own or preferably with a colleague(s).

Major Ofsted framework headings	Features of high-quality PE and school sport in your school	Indicate which DfES outcomes these relate to (1–10)	Tick if there is sufficient evidence to make judgement.	Tick if more evidence is needed and state what more needs to be
In relation to learners' achievement and standards:				
In relation to learners' personal development:				
In relation to teaching and learning:				

Unit 1: Introduction to Self-evaluation

1.6 Collecting and Analysing Key Sources of Evidence

This section gives an overview of the key sources of evidence needed in order to answer the basic questions for each section of the framework:

- How well are we doing?

- What are the priorities for improvement?

Methods of collecting key sources of evidence for self-evaluation:

- Evaluation of learners' performance indicators:
  - analysis of GCSE and A-level exams using the Autumn package and PANDA (Individual school PANDA [Performance and Assessment Report] and the document that provides national figures for all attainment measures included within the School Improvement Summary Report section will soon be available for all schools to download from the PANDA website – see the school PANDA for details.)
  - teacher assessments using the Autumn package at KS 3
  - teacher assessments at FS, KS 1 and KS 2
  - teacher assessments against HQPESS
  - use of YELLIS systems to check added value at GCSE
  - use of LEA added value systems for GCSE
  - use of Fisher Family Trust systems of value added for whole school picture

- Analysis of learners' participation in lessons

- Analysis of learners' participation in extra-curricular activities

- Observation of lessons

- Scrutiny of learners' work

- Discussions with learners

- Discussions with teachers

- Use of surveys and consultation with parents, learners and staff

- Discussions with community stakeholders.

Units 2 and 3 take participants through how to use these methods of collecting evidence and to analyse the findings against the criteria of the Ofsted framework for inspection and the DfES criteria for HQPESS.

For specific examples of collecting evidence, refer to:

- 'Do you have High Quality PE and Sport in your School?' (DfES, 2005)

- 'The National PESS Professional Development Programme', with special reference to:
  - the Evaluate to Inform and Improve SD/Q Delegate Workbook – Secondary – 2005
  - the Evaluate to Inform and Improve PD/Q Delegate Workbook – Primary – 2005

1.7 Keeping an Overview of Findings from Self-evaluation Activity and Building a Manageable Plan of Self-evaluation Activity

Throughout the training, you need to keep an overview or aide-memoire of what you have found out by carrying out self-evaluation activities.

At the same time, start to consider how to build a **manageable plan of self-evaluation activity**.

- The self-evaluation activities should **not be too burdensome** in terms of time and energy.
- The plan should **involve all staff and personnel involved in teaching PESS** in your setting.
- There should be a **specific focus** to each part of the plan arising from what is already known about the standards and provision in the subject.
- The plan of self-evaluation activity should relate closely to the subject/school improvement/development plan and include **monitoring of the subject/school's priorities.**

Below is an example of an outline planning schedule for monitoring of learners' activity, taken from 'The National PESS Professional Development Programme Modules PD/Q and SD/Q: Evaluate to Inform and Improve' (Handout 1).

The plan below was drawn up in response to the subject leader wishing to investigate how much time individual learners spent being active.

Monitoring method	When will this take place?	How often will this take place?	What information will you seek? How will it be recorded?	How will you use the information?	What difference might you expect to see as a result of acquiring the information?
1. Talk with learners	During tutor time	Once every half-term	Minutes spent active. Weekly activity log/diary	Feedback to relevant people (eg teachers of PESS, subject leader, head teacher, parents)	Changes to curriculum planning, learner awareness, staff and parent awareness
2.					
3.					

In Unit 4, you will draw up an improvement plan to include a manageable plan of self-evaluation activity.

Unit 1: Introduction to Self-evaluation

Task 8 (30 minutes) – Ongoing throughout each unit

Keep an overview of issues arising from self-evaluation activities and build a manageable plan of self-evaluation activities.

Working on your own or preferably with a colleague(s), use the template (Table 2) below to keep notes of the issues arising from each self-evaluation activity carried out as you work through the course.

The information in this form (Table 2) should help you to build an overview of the evidence and evaluations you can draw on in preparation for writing the SEF. You can use the table below as a notepad as you work through the units.

Table 2: An overview of self-evaluation activity

Key sources of evidence/ self-evaluation activities	When these activities might take place	Strengths Indicate which part of the SEF they will inform i.e. Achievement & standards (AS), Personal development/Every Child Matters (PD ECM), Teaching and Learning Curriculum, Guidance and support, Leadership and management.	Areas for improvement Indicate which part of the SEF they will inform Identify **priorities** to be taken forward to the action plan – **P**

Unit 2: Evaluating Learners' Standards, Achievement, Personal Development and Well-being in Physical Education

Purpose and Aims

Participants will become more familiar with recognising the criteria for high-quality physical education and school sport and links to the Ofsted common inspection schedule, including 'Every Child Matters'.

This unit is about answering the question, 'How well are we doing?' It will prepare leaders to make rigorous judgements about learners' standards, progress, achievement, personal development and well-being.

This unit also helps leaders and teachers to answer the question, 'How do we know how well we are doing?' by using a range of evidence to make rigorous judgements about standards, progress, achievement, personal development and well-being in physical education and school sport.

The evidence to be used includes observation of lessons, analysis of learners' examination results and teachers' assessments, discussions with learners and analysis of written work.

Participants will practise applying the criteria rigorously and recording their findings. They will evaluate their findings and write a report for the SEF. There will be a strong focus on inclusion in all activities to reflect the principles underpinning 'Every Child Matters'.

Participants will identify strengths and areas for improvement to take forward into development planning.

Unit 2 Learning Outcomes

By the end of this unit, participants will be able to:
- understand the criteria for evaluating learners' standards, progress, achievement and personal development
- recognise key sources of evidence
- evaluate learners' standards, progress, achievement and personal development accurately using a range of evidence
- record judgements about standards, progress, achievement and personal development clearly, accurately and unambiguously
- write an evaluation of standards, progress, achievement, personal development and well-being for the SEF
- identify areas for improvement and plan relevant monitoring and evaluation activity.

Requirements

You will need:
- 'Every Child Matters: Framework for the Inspection of Schools in England' (Ofsted, 2005)
- a school Self-evaluation Form (SEF)
- 'High Quality PE and Sport for Young People' (DfES, 2004)
- *A Guide to Self-review in Physical Education* (baalpe, 2006)

- 'Guidance for the Inspection of Schools: Using the Evaluation Schedule' (Ofsted, 2005) Ref: HMI 2504
- 'Guidance for the Inspection of Schools: Conducting the Inspection' (Ofsted, 2005) Ref: HMI 2502
- *Achieving Excellence* (baalpe, 2004)
- QCA DVD materials or ACCAC video materials for National Curriculum Levels at KS 1, 2 and 3
- *Assessment for Learning in Physical Education* (baalpe, 2005)
- Appendix II in 'Inspecting Subjects 3–11: Physical Education' (Ofsted, 2000) pp 88–92
- 'Inspecting Subjects 11–16: Physical Education with Guidance on self-evaluation' (Ofsted, 2001)
- 'Inspecting Subjects Post-16: Physical Education with Guidance on Self-evaluation' (Ofsted, 2001).

Unit Development

2.1 What Do We Mean by 'Achievement', 'Standards' and 'Progress'?
2.1.1 Questions raised in the school Self-evaluation Form (SEF) on achievement and standards
2.1.2 What do we mean by 'Learners' Achievement and Progress'?
2.1.3 What do we mean by 'Learners' Standards in Physical Education'?

2.2 Identifying Key Sources of Evidence for Evaluating Learners' Standards, Progress and Achievement

2.3 Using Data and Assessment to Identify Strengths and Weaknesses in Standards, Progress and Achievement

2.4 Using Other Sources of Evidence to Evaluate Standards, Achievement and Progress

2.5 What Do We Mean by 'Learners' Personal Development and Well-being in Physical Education'?
2.5 1 Questions raised in the SEF on personal development and well-being
2.5.2 What do we mean by 'Personal Development and Well-being in Physical Education'?

2.6 Identifying Key Sources of Evidence for Learners' Personal Development and Well-being

2.7 Observing Learners in Lessons: Identifying the Achievement, Progress, Standards and Personal Development of Different Groups of Learners

2.8 Using Other Sources of Evidence to Evaluate Learners' Standards, Progress, Achievement and Personal Development

2.9 Evaluating Findings and Writing a Report for the SEF

Table 3: Summary of tasks for Unit 2

	Task 9 (20 minutes) Optional Task	Identify the key sources of evidence on which to base evaluation of learners' standards and achievement. Identify where you have gathered evidence and evaluated it. What did it tell you? Identify where you need to spend more time gathering evidence and evaluating it.
	Pre-course Task 10 (60 minutes) Secondary only	Analyse data in your school.
	Pre-course Task 11 (40 minutes) Primary or Secondary	Analyse learners' progress through teachers' assessments.
	Task 12 (20 minutes) Optional Task	Where do we find the evidence for learners' personal development and well-being?
	Task 13 (15 minutes)	Identify three strengths and two weaknesses in learners' personal development and well-being in physical education in your own setting. How do you know this? Do you need to find out more?
	Pre-course Task 14 (15 minutes)	Participants are to have viewed the information on the DVD about the primary school and the Year 6 lesson prior to the course and have read the information in Appendix I.
	Task 15 (45 minutes)	Evaluate progress and personal development in a Year 6 lesson.
	Mid-course Task 16 (45 minutes)	Use a range of evidence to evaluate standards, progress, achievement and personal development.
	Mid-course Task 17 (60 minutes)	Write the section of the SEF for standards and achievement, personal development and well-being.

2.1 What Do We Mean by 'Achievement', 'Standards' and 'Progress'?

2.1.1 Questions raised in the school Self-evaluation Form (SEF) on achievement and standards

The Self-evaluation Form (SEF), Section 3, on Achievement and Standards asks the following questions:

> 3. How well do learners achieve?
>
> 3a. What are learners achieving and what is the standard of their work?
> • The standards learners reach as indicated by their test and examination results; any significant variations between groups of learners, subjects, courses and key stages; trends over time; comparisons with other schools; whether learners reach challenging targets.
>
> • The standards of current work in relation to their learning goals (noting any significant differences between current work and recent results).
>
> • Learners' progress relative to their starting points and capabilities, with any significant variations between groups of learners – making clear whether there are any groups underachieving.
>
> 3c. On the basis of your evaluation, what are your key priorities for development?

We therefore need to ensure that we understand the terms used for achievement, standards and progress, and the criteria that are used to evaluate them.

We need to know what key sources of evidence to gather in order to answer the questions in the SEF, and what criteria to use in coming to an overall evaluation.

2.1.2 What do we mean by 'Learners' Achievement and Progress'?

The judgement on learners' **achievement** is an overall evaluation of how well learners are doing in school, both in terms of the standards they reach and, importantly, in terms of the **progress** they make, taking into account their prior attainment and their capabilities.

In order to judge how well learners are achieving, you need to ask several questions:
• Have learners made the progress you would expect for their age?

• Taking into account their starting point (prior attainment) and their potential (contextual factors such as gender, socio-economic circumstances, EAL, SEN), are the standards reached by these learners high enough?

• Taking into account the contextual factors for these learners, is this progress what is expected, better than that or worse?

Any differences in the progress and achievement of different groups of learners should be identified and any underachievement recognised. This must lead to action to improve standards for those learners.

Different groups include: girls; boys; learners of differing abilities, including learners with learning disabilities and/or difficulties; gifted and talented learners; minority ethnic groups; learners whose first language is not English; learners from refugee or asylum-seeking families; learners from traveller families and 'looked after' learners.

Familiarise yourself with the criteria and benchmarks for 'How Well do Learners Achieve in PE?' in *A Guide to Self-review in Physical Education* (baalpe, 2006) and Ofsted's 'Guidance for the Inspection of Schools: Using the Evaluation Schedule' (2005).

2.1.3 What do we mean by 'Learners' Standards in Physical Education'?

Judgements on the standards learners reach compare learners' performance to that expected nationally, whether this is compared to National Curriculum levels or examination results, or other course requirements. Participants need to be familiar with the expected standards for National Curriculum and/or examination courses.

Schools should have information/data that throws light on the standards reached by **different groups** of learners (eg boys/girls/minority ethnic groups/learners of differing abilities/SEN learners – see above). It is important that, in analysing standards, these groups are identified. Which groups are doing well and which groups are underachieving?

The expectation is that a clear evaluation of standards and achievement is given, with reference to the evidence used, but avoiding tables and descriptive information.

In order to judge standards, use records of teacher assessments or examination data to ask the following questions:

• Are learners performing as you would expect for their age, better than that or worse?

• Have you taken into account the level descriptors of the National Curriculum and non-statutory QCA guidance?

  • How well are learners doing across the four strands of the National Curriculum? How well are they:
    – acquiring and developing skills?
    – evaluating and improving?
    – selecting and applying?
    – acquiring knowledge and understanding of fitness and health?

  • How good are learners' key skills in:
    – communication – reading, writing, speaking and listening?
    – application of number?
    – information and communication technology?
    – working with others?
    – improving own learning and performance?
    – problem solving?

  • How good are learners' thinking skills in:
    – information processing?
    – reasoning?
    – enquiry?
    – creative thinking?
    – evaluation?

Suggested reading:

- QCA DVD materials or ACCAC video materials for National Curriculum Levels at KS 1, 2 and 3.

- *Assessment for Learning in Physical Education* (baalpe, 2005).

- The National PESS Professional Development Programme SD/Q and PD/Q Evaluate to Inform and Improve.

- The National PESS Professional Development Programme PD/H and SD/H Assessing Progress and Attainments in PE.

- 'How Well do Learners Achieve in PE?' in *A Guide to Self-review in Physical Education* (baalpe, 2006).

- 'The National Curriculum Handbook for Primary Teachers in England: Key Stages 1 and 2' (DfES/QCA, 1999).

- 'The National Curriculum Handbook for Secondary Teachers in England: Key Stages 3 and 4' (DfES/QCA, 1999).

2.2 Identifying Key Sources of Evidence for Evaluating Learners' Standards, Progress and Achievement

Where is the evidence for standards, progress and achievement? The following task helps to consider where and how to collect the evidence to enable an accurate judgement on standards, progress and achievement to be made.

Task 9 (20 minutes) – Optional

• Identify the key sources of evidence on which to base evaluations of learners' standards, progress and achievement.

• Identify where you have gathered evidence and evaluated it. What did it tell you?

• Identify where you need to spend more time gathering evidence and evaluating it.

Work on your own or with a colleague(s).

Key sources of evidence for learners' standards, progress and achievement	Identify where you have gathered evidence and evaluated it. What did it tell you?(ie areas of strength, areas for improvement)	Do you need to spend more time gathering this type of evidence?

Key sources of evidence for learners' standards, progress and achievement include:

- gathering national data in tests and examinations to compare your school's performance with others (secondary only)

- analysing teachers' assessments to compare your school's performance with others (KS 3 only)

- observing learners at work in lessons ***

- analysing surveys of learners' involvement in extra-curricular activities and activities beyond the school

- analysing registers/attendance records in physical education lessons

- analysing learners' own assessments

- observing playgrounds

- talking to learners

- talking to parents

- talking to teachers

- analysing learners' written work.

*** When observing a single lesson, it is not always possible to judge standards and achievement. It is possible to judge progress. (See Ofsted's 'Guidance on the Use of Evidence Forms' (July 2005, p 2). However, it is possible to judge standards in a particular feature of physical education, for example, by observing a wider range of lessons across a number of classes and using other evidence from talking to pupils and teachers' assessments to triangulate the evaluation.

2.3 Using Data and Assessment to Identify Strengths and Weaknesses in Standards, Progress and Achievement

What data can we usefully analyse in PE and school sport to help raise standards and achievement?

- Examination data.
- Teacher assessments.
- Registers of attendance and participation in lessons.
- Participation in out-of-lesson learning/activity, both within and beyond the school.

You can analyse data to find out about **standards** by looking for:

- comparisons with national averages for all learners across the country

- upward or downward trends from year to year

- how boys and girls compare with boys and girls across the country

- whether the standards reached by many different groups of learners vary (see 2.1.2).

Key sources of evidence:

- End of key stage teacher assessments.

- GCSE results or equivalent.

- GCE A-level results.

- Comparisons with national figures for all learners, for boys and for girls are available in the PANDA for your school.

- Comparisons with own and neighbouring LEA data.

- Comparisons with other sports colleges.

- JSLA and CSLA achievements.

- NGB awards achieved.

You can analyse data to find out about **achievement and progress** by looking for:

- value added from a baseline start point to an end of key stage assessment or GCSE grade result (ie whether learners have made the progress expected nationally, better than that or worse)

- whether learners met the targets expected of them, when targets have been set on the basis of their prior attainment or capability

- how well learners achieved in physical education compared to the other subjects they took at GCSE or A-level – Relative Performance Indicator (RPI).

Always look for differences between different groups of learners (as identified in 2.1.2).

Schools use many different ways of analysing learners' standards, results, assessment and achievement. It is important that you find out and understand how your school analyses results and learners' progress, and work with your senior leaders on the common approach in your school.

They may use any of the following to analyse results:

- Pupil Achievement Tracker – www.standards.dfes.gov.uk/performance/pat

- Fisher Family Trust

- PANDA

- LEA analysis

- Autumn package – Ofsted

- MIDYIS

- YELLIS

- ALIS.

Further guidance on analysis of examination results and teachers' assessments is available in:

- Ofsted training:

  – *Interpreting Data* CD-ROM (Ofsted, April 2005)

  – 'Training for School Inspection 2005: Data Module' (Ofsted, August 2005)

- 'The National PESS Professional Development Programme Modules PD/Q and SD/ Q: Evaluate to Inform and Improve' (DfES, 2005).

Pre-course Task 10 (60 minutes) – Secondary Only

This task deals with analysing data in your school. Select either Key Stage 3 teacher assessments for current Year 9 learners or GCSE or A-level results, and use the following questions to analyse your data.

To analyse **standards**, ask the questions:

1. How do the results/teacher assessments compare with national averages for all learners?

2. Is there any trend upward or downward from year to year?

3. How do boys and girls compare with each other and with boys and girls across the country?

4. Do standards reached by different groups of learners vary? (See 2.1.2.)

To analyse **progress and achievement**, ask the questions:

5. What is the value added for individuals and for groups (ie have learners made better or worse progress than that expected nationally)?

6. Have learners met the targets expected of them?

7. How well have learners achieved in physical education compared to their other subjects? (Relative Performance Indicator – RPI.)

8. Are there any significant differences between groups of learners?

Work on your own or with a colleague(s), preferably a senior leader responsible for data analysis.

Analysis of Standards

1. How do the results/teacher assessments compare with national averages for all learners?	
2. Is there any trend upward or downward from year to year?	
3. How do boys and girls compare with each other and with boys and girls across the country?	
4. Do standards reached by different groups of learners vary? (See 2.1.2.)	

Analysis of Progress and Achievement

5. What is the value added for individuals and for groups (ie have learners made better or worse progress than that expected nationally)?	
6. Have learners met the targets expected of them?	
7. How well have learners achieved in physical education compared to their other subjects? (Relative Performance Indicator – RPI.)	
8. Are there any significant differences between groups of learners?	

Pre-course Task 11 (40 minutes) – Primary or Secondary

This task deals with analysing learners' progress through teachers' assessments.

Strengths		Areas for improvement	
Proportion of learners achieving **higher** standards than expected	Specific areas of strength in learners' knowledge, skills and understanding	Proportion of learners achieving **lower** standards than expected	Specific areas of weakness in learners' knowledge, skills and understanding
Issues arising leading to plans for action and professional development:		Issues arising leading to plans for action and professional development:	

Unit 2: Evaluating Learners' Standards, Achievement,
Personal Development and Well-being in Physical Education

2.4 Using Other Sources of Evidence to Evaluate Standards, Achievement and Progress

By the very nature of an active subject such as physical education, we need to look at more ways of finding out about learners' progress and achievement than by analysing data on examination performance and teachers' assessment. The analysis of data is explored in Section 2.3 but, in this section, we are still answering the question **how do we know** how well learners are achieving?

Well-focused, direct observation of learners at work in lessons can be an effective means of monitoring and evaluating progress, as can be seen in the example given below.

> ### Example – Secondary 11–16 High School
>
> #### Question/focus – How well are we doing?
> The HoD wanted to find out about how well the learners were making progress in PE. He was uncertain whether they were using the best curriculum model, which included six-week units of work.
>
> #### Monitoring activity – How do we know?
> The HoD and his second in the department made focused visits to lessons at the beginning and end of units of work (Lesson 1 and Lesson 6), focusing on the progress of three learners and noting differences in their progress and personal development in relation to the learning objectives for the units and NC levels of attainment. This was carried out for one class in each activity in each year group, ensuring that all the teachers were included. By including the second in the department/head teacher in the activity, the HoD/subject leader ensured that all staff, including the subject leader, were included. The approach was discussed with the whole department and at least one of the observations was also used for the purpose of individual teacher performance management – which included a departmental focus on the achievement of learners.
>
> #### Evaluation – How well are we doing?
> The outcome of the monitoring was analysed. Though the progress was judged to be satisfactory, the HoD was not satisfied with this, and set higher expectations of good progress.
>
> #### Action to follow – What do we need to do to improve?
> It was deemed necessary to set up pilot groups that followed 8- and 10-week units of work in games, and to pilot the running of gymnastics and dance units one after the other in order to try to establish progression and continuity in the common elements linking the two activities.

This is an example of well-focused self-evaluation activity that involved all teachers in the department. It resulted in action to bring about improvement. The next stage would be to carry out further checks on learners' progress for the pilot groups in order to determine the effect of increasing the length of the units of work on learners' key outcomes.

2.5 What Do We Mean by 'Learners' Personal Development and Well-being in Physical Education'?

2.5.1 Questions raised in the SEF on personal development and well-being

Section 4 on personal development and well-being on the self-evaluation form (SEF) asks the questions:

4. How good is the overall personal development and well-being of the learners?

4a. To what extent do learners adopt healthy lifestyles?

4b. To what extent do learners feel safe and adopt safe practices?

4c. How much do learners enjoy their education?

4d. How well do learners make a positive contribution to the community?

4e. How well do learners prepare for their future economic well-being?

4g. On the basis of your evaluation, what are your key priorities for development?

2.5.2 What do we mean by 'Personal Development and Well-being in Physical Education'?

Refresh your understanding of the criteria for the Ofsted 'Every Child Matters' and how they relate to the DfES outcomes for 'High Quality Physical Education and School Sport' in the overview on pages 10-14.

The **desired outcomes of learners' development and well-being** are that learners:

- have good attendance for PE

- behave well in PE lessons

- enjoy their lessons and have a positive attitude towards PE and sport

- have the confidence to get involved in PE and school sport

- have a desire to improve and achieve in relation to their own abilities

- take full part in PE lessons

- willingly take part in a range of competitive, creative and challenge-type activities

- think about and make appropriate decisions for themselves

- take adequate physical exercise and understand how to live a healthy lifestyle

- feel safe from bullying and racist incidents

- have the confidence to talk to staff and others when at risk

- express their views and take part in communal activities

- develop skills and personal qualities that will enable them to achieve future economic well-being (eg basic skills of communication, numeracy and ICT)

- understand career options and acquire workplace skills

- develop spiritually, morally, socially and culturally.

For criteria and judgements related to PE for personal development, refer to your completed copy of *A Guide to Self-review in Physical Education* (baalpe, 2006) and 'Guidance for the Inspection of Schools: Using the Evaluation Schedule' (Ofsted 2005).

2.6 Identifying Key Sources of Evidence for Learners' Personal Development and Well-being

Task 12 (20 minutes) – Optional

This task deals with where to find the evidence for learners' personal development and well-being. Working on your own or with a colleague(s), identify sources of evidence for each section, referring back to the national criteria for high-quality outcomes defined by the DfES and Ofsted on pages 10–14 in the overview. Indicate where one source of evidence can be used for more than one section.

'Every Child Matters' Criteria	Sources of evidence
To what extent do learners adopt healthy lifestyles?	
To what extent do learners feel safe and adopt safe practices?	
How much do learners enjoy their education?	
How well do learners make a positive contribution to the community?	
How well do learners prepare for their future economic well-being?	

Task 13 (15 minutes)

Work on your own or with a colleague(s).

- Using the criteria set out in Unit 1 for the Ofsted 'Every Child Matters' and the DfES 'High Quality Physical Education in School Sport', identify three strengths and two weaknesses in learners' personal development and well-being in physical education in your own setting.
- How do you know this?
- Do you need to find out more?

Strengths in personal development and well-being	How do you know? (ie What evidence do you have for this?)	Do you need to find out more and how might you do this?

Weaknesses in personal development and well-being	How do you know? (ie What evidence do you have for this?)	Do you need to find out more and how might you do this?

Unit 2: Evaluating Learners' Standards, Achievement, Personal Development and Well-being in Physical Education

Key sources of evidence for learners' personal development and well-being:

- Attendance records.
- Participation registers for lessons, extra-curricular activities and other sport-related activities.
- Learners' views on provision.
- Observation of lessons and other activities.

2.7 Observing Learners in Lessons: Identifying the Achievement, Progress, Standards and Personal Development of Different Groups of Learners

Pre-course Task 14 (15 minutes)

Participants are to have viewed the information on the DVD (and have read the information in Appendix 1) about the primary school and the Year 6 lesson prior to the course.

Task 15 (45 minutes) Primary, secondary and special

This task looks at evaluating progress and personal development in a Year 6 lesson.

Working on your own or with a colleague(s), observe the Year 6 lesson on gymnastics from the 35-minute chapter point to the end of the lesson.

Progress – Write down what progress the pupils make in the four strands of the National Curriculum and elements of HQPESS. Is it what you would expect for pupils of this age and capability?
Standards – Can you make any evaluation of the standards demonstrated in relation to National Curriculum criteria?
Groups – Note any differences between the progress and standards of the different ability groups.
Personal development and well-being – including 'Every Child Matters' criteria – Make any evaluation you can, with reference to the evidence.

Summary of Judgements

	Progress	**Personal development and well-being**
Girls		
Boys		
Higher-attaining learners		
Mid-attaining learners		
Low-attaining learners		

2.8 Using Other Sources of Evidence to Evaluate Learners' Achievement, Standards, Progress and Personal Development

Though observation of lessons will always be an important way of finding out how well learners are doing in physical education, other surveys and discussions can help to inform your evaluation.

1. Analysing registers/attendance records in physical education lessons and extra-curricular activities.

2. Observing playgrounds.

3. Talking to learners.

4. Talking to parents.

5. Talking to teachers.

6. Analysing learners' written work.

1 Analysing Registers/Attendance Records in Physical Education Lessons and Extra-curricular Activities

- Keep records of learners' involvement in lessons, extra-curricular activities and other out-of-school activities.

- Analyse the involvement of different groups of learners.

- Observe the activities and evaluate their impact on learners' progress and achievement.

Primary/secondary – Analysis of participation rates in lessons

An indication of pupils' attitudes, interest and motivation towards physical education and school sport can be found in an analysis of the pupils taking part or not taking part in lessons.

Use the table given below to help identify where pupils' levels of participation are high or low. Ask class teachers to complete the table.

Consider the reasons for this.

Use this analysis as the basis for questions to pupils and students.

Numbers of Pupils Not Taking Part in Lessons Over One Term/Unit of Work/Year

Year Group	Games		Gymnastics		Dance		Swimming		Athletics	
	Boys	Girls	Boys	Girls	Boys	Girls	Boys	Girls	Boys	Girls
Fdn/7										
1/8										
2/9										
3/10										
4/11										
5/12										
6/13										

Reasons for Non-participation

Summary/issues to take to table 2: An Overview of Self-evaluation Activity

Strengths:

Areas for development:

Primary/Secondary – Analysis of Participation in Extra-curricular Activities

An indication of pupils' attitudes, interest and motivation towards physical education and school sport can be found in an analysis of the pupils' participation in extra-curricular activities. This information can be gathered weekly, termly or annually.

Numbers of Pupils Taking Part in Activities Over One Term/Unit of Work/Year

Year Group	Football		Netball		Gymnastics		Dance		Swimming		Other	
	Boys	Girls	Boys	Girls	Boys	Girls	Boys	Girls	Boys	Girls	Boys	Girls
Fdn/7												
1/8												
2/9												
3/10												
4/11												
5/12												
6/13												

Summary/issues to take to table 2: An Overview of Self-evaluation Activity

Strengths:

Areas for development:

Unit 2: Evaluating Learners' Standards, Achievement, Personal Development and Well-being in Physical Education

55

2 Observing Playgrounds

Observe activity in playgrounds. Use the criteria for standards, achievement and progress, personal development and well-being alongside those for HQPESS.

Record your findings, taking particular note of the levels of activity, enjoyment and cooperation of different groups of pupils. Compare with your own and other teachers' assessments of learners.

3 Talking to Learners

It is becoming increasingly important to find out learners' views of their experiences. These can be sought through regular surveys or through discussions.

Evidence of standard, progress and achievement, pupils' attitudes and personal development and the quality of teaching can be gained through well-structured discussions with pupils.

Talking to pupils can take place informally, as part of lesson observation or can be arranged formally.

When arranging formal discussions, choose a small sample of pupils to talk to who are representative of the different groups in the school. You may wish to focus on the end of each key stage.

If using questioning of pupils to find out about **standards**, ensure that you are fully familiar with the national expectations for the age group and are aware of what they have been taught.

Use earlier evidence gathered to provide a focus for discussions (eg if lesson observations had highlighted a weakness in knowledge and understanding of health and fitness).

Focus on specific groups of pupils if there is evidence of underachievement in those groups (eg girls, higher-attaining pupils).

Focus on specific groups of pupils where inclusion may be an issue (eg where there are high numbers of non-participating pupils, ensure that a number of these pupils are included in your sample).

Questionnaires can be devised around pertinent issues and used across larger groups of pupils. These should become a regular feature of consultation and self-review.

In formal discussions, take time to enable pupils to relax and settle by asking general questions about their experiences in PE and school sport.

Ensure that ground rules are firmly established so that pupils understand that no individual, whether a teacher or pupil, should be named.

The approach to confidentiality within child-protection guidelines should be understood by teachers and pupils.

Questions for Pupils/Students on Teaching, Learning and Attitudes	
Year group:	Ability:	Gender:

Question	Pupils' Response
Which lessons are most interesting/enjoyable and why?	
Which lessons are least interesting/enjoyable and why?	
How hard do you have to work in lessons? What are the differences between lessons?	
What activities in lessons help you to learn and improve?	
How do you know what you have to do to improve?	
Do you know how well you are doing in PE? How?	
Which PE and sport-related activities out of lesson time do you take part in?	
Are there any additional extra-curricular activities that you would like to see put on in the school?	

Summary of Strengths and Weaknesses
(Include issues to transfer onto Table 2: An Overview of Self-evaluation Activity)

Strengths:	Areas for improvement:

See also:

- the questions in the Ofsted pupils' questionnaires, available on the Ofsted website (www.ofsted.gov.uk)
- sample questions to pupils in Ofsted's 'Inspecting Subjects 3–11: Physical Education' (2000) (p 88).

4 Talking to Parents

All schools arrange regular contact with parents, most often to report on pupils' progress. It can be useful to use times of direct contact with parents to seek their views on the provision of PE and sport in the school.

Other means of consultation with parents may already be in place, such as annual questionnaires, and all that is needed is the addition of well-focused questions relating to issues in physical education. Consider using the questionnaire below as the basis for consultation, making adjustments to suit your school and the emerging issues.

Parents' Views on the Provision of PE and School Sport					
Statements	Strongly Agree	Agree	Disagree	Strongly Disagree	Don't Know
1. My child enjoys PE lessons.					
Comment:					
2. My child enjoys sport and other PE-related activities provided out of school hours.					
Comment:					
3. I am happy with the standards my child achieves in PE and school sport.					
Comment:					
4. I am happy with the quality of the teaching in my child's lessons.					
Comment:					
5. I am happy with the range of activities taught in PE lessons.					
Comment:					
6. I am happy with the range of PE and sporting activities provided out of lesson time.					
Comment:					
7. What do you like most about the provision for PE and sport?	Comment:				
8. What would you like to change?	Comment:				
Parents' responses should be analysed and the emerging issues recorded to add to the overview of self-evaluation/review activities. Use the table below to record emerging strengths and areas for improvement. Transfer this information to Table 2.					

<table>
<tr><td colspan="2" align="center">Summary of Strengths and Weaknesses
(Include issues to transfer onto Table 2: An Overview of Self-evaluation Activity)</td></tr>
<tr><td>Strengths:</td><td>Areas for improvement:</td></tr>
</table>

5 Talking to Teachers

An effective school involves all staff in self-review and evaluation. The review can be at a number of levels:

• Class teacher review of individual lessons/units of work – the focus is likely to be on pupils' standards, progress, achievement and the effectiveness of teaching.

• Teacher review of areas of responsibility – the focus is on standards, progress and achievement across the subject, teaching and learning across the subject, and features of management such as professional development, curriculum planning, resources and staffing.

Views can be sought verbally through regular meetings of subject/year group/whole staff, although questionnaires may result in a more considered response.

Not all staff need to be included. Samples can be taken and the nature of the sample can be guided by issues emerging through other self-evaluation/review activities.

Consider consulting all staff involved in providing PE or sporting activities, whether it be lunchtime supervisors or coaches.

The following questions can be used:

Questions for Teachers/Staff to Review Individual Lessons/Units of Work	
Details of the lesson/unit: Year group: G/B/M: Number in group: Learning outcomes: Other context:	
Standards, Achievement and Progress	**Yes or No? Why?**
1. Did **all** the pupils achieve the lesson's objectives?	
2. Did any pupils make better progress than expected?	
3. Did any pupils make less progress than expected?	
Teaching and Learning	
4. What worked well in the lesson and why?	
5. Did anything not work well that could be improved next time?	
Further comments:	
Summarise responses and transfer issues arising to Table 2.	
Summary of Strengths and Weaknesses	
(Include issues to transfer onto Table 2: An Overview of Self-evaluation Activity)	
Strengths:	Areas for improvement:

Questions For Teachers/Staff to Review Areas of Responsibility	
Areas of responsibility:	

Standards, Achievement and Progress	Comment
1. Which pupils are achieving well and why?	
2. Are there any groups of pupils that are not achieving as well as they should and why?	

Teaching and Learning	
3. What features of teaching are working well and are readily adopted across the subject/ department?	
4. What features of teaching need to be improved across the subject/department?	

Management	
5. How have any self-evaluation/review activities affected pupils' standards in the subject and the quality of the teaching and learning?	
6. In what ways have the performance-management arrangements benefited the subject/department?	
7. What has been the impact of staff-development activities on the quality of teaching and learning?	

Questions For Teachers/Staff to Review Areas of Responsibility (continued)	
8. Are there any issues relating to the breadth, balance and relevance of the curriculum planning that affect how well pupils achieve and learn? (Consider using a curriculum analysis such as those provided in the Active Mark/Sports Mark Award applications.)	
9. Describe any issues relating to staff deployment that affect how well pupils achieve and learn.	
10. Describe any issues concerning resources and accommodation that affect how well pupils achieve and learn.	
11. In what ways has the subject/department improved most in the last two years?	
12. What features does the subject/department need to improve?	
13. Are there any other concerns affecting how well pupils achieve and learn?	

Summary of Strengths and Weaknesses
(Include issues to transfer onto Table 2: An Overview of Self-evaluation Activity)

Strengths:	Areas for improvement:

6 Analysing Learners' Written Work

This task is applicable to secondary schools with pupils and students involved in examination work.

Purpose

A great deal can be learnt about the level of pupils'/students' standards, their attitudes and the quality of teaching and learning by looking more closely at their written work and applying the criteria for high-quality standards, teaching and learning.

Sample

The selection of a sample of pupils'/students' written work will depend on a number of factors:

- Whether a sample across specific groups is required. Consider the inclusion of pupils of different ability, backgrounds and gender.

- Whether there is a focus to this activity as a result of previous self-evaluation.

Suggested sample:

- Select three students from a Year 11 or Year 13 examination cohort who exemplify higher, average and lower attainment and reflect a good spread across the various backgrounds of pupils.

- Choose a common piece of work that pupils/students undertook at the beginning of the previous year and the most recent piece of work.

Analysis

Use the pro forma overleaf to help to identify the key strengths and areas for improvement emerging from your analysis. Transfer the issues arising to Table 2: An Overview of Self-evaluation Activity in Unit 1.

Analysis of Learners' Written Work		
Year group:	Ability:	Gender:

Context of the work:

- Learning outcomes
- Unit of work

Criteria for High-quality Written	Evaluation
Attitudes and Personal Development	
• Do pupils complete tasks set, including corrections? • Is there evidence of re-drafting of written work reflecting a commitment to improvement? • Do pupils persevere with tasks? • Is work well organised?	
Standards, Achievement and Progress	
• Is the work legible and presented with a concern for layout and appearance? • Is it easy for the reader to follow, with a shape that gives it coherence? • Are arguments well developed? • Do pupils make progress (eg the work they do now is better than the work they did last year)? • Does pupils' written work show improvement in the quality of the content, structure, punctuation, spelling, grammar and handwriting? • Are mathematical or scientific processes lucid? • Is language precise? • Are illustrations clear and accurate? • Do pupils adopt an appropriate style to match the purpose of the writing? • Are illustrations clear and accurate?	

Analysis of Learners' Written Work (continued)

- Do pupils use various means for conveying information (words, graphs, maps, statistics etc)?

- Are illustrations clear and accurate?

- Do pupils use various means for conveying information (words, graphs, maps, statistics etc)?

- At what level/grade are pupils in their knowledge, skills and understanding, in relation to GCSE/AS/A-level?

- Are all pupils progressing as well as they should be?

Teaching and Assessment

- Is the work marked regularly, with appropriate annotations?

- Does the work show improvements related to the comments made in previous marking?

- Are pupils told what progress they are making with their written work?

- Are pupils given specific achievable targets?

- Are tasks appropriate for the age and attainment of pupils (ie are expectations high enough)?

- Is good attention paid to developing pupils' literacy, numeracy and ICT skills?

Summary of Strengths and Weaknesses

(Include issues to transfer onto Table 2: An Overview of Self-evaluation Activity)

Strengths:	Areas for improvement:

Mid-course Task 16 (45 minutes)

This task focuses on using a range of evidence to evaluate standards, achievement, progress and personal development.

Working on your own or with a colleague(s):

- choose one or more of the above means of gathering evidence on learners' standards, achievement and personal development
- decide on a focus for the surveys/questions/analysis
- decide on how often these activities should be carried out and build this into a plan for self-evaluation activity
- transfer strengths and weaknesses to Table 2: An Overview of Self-evaluation Activity.

2.9 Evaluating Findings and Writing a Report for the SEF

You need to complete a school Self-evaluation Form for your subject. You need to remind yourself of the criteria for writing a good SEF (see Unit 1).

A good SEF should:

- convey a clear picture of how well the subject/school is doing
- provide proof of how you know what you know
- show what you are doing to build on successes and remedy weaknesses.

Look to:

- provide clear judgements based on the framework criteria
- provide judgements that are supported by a good range of key evidence
- ensure strengths, weaknesses and priorities for improvement are clearly identified
- make links between issues raised in the Achievement section and how the school is tackling these in the sections on Provision and Leadership and Management.

Look at the special school and the secondary school examples of completed sections of the SEF on Achievement and Standards and Personal Development in Unit 1.

Look at the example of a completed secondary school SEF in Appendix III.

Mid-course Task 17 (60 minutes)

Working on your own or with a colleague(s), write the section of the SEF for Standards and Achievement, Personal Development and Well-being.

Unit 3: Evaluating the Impact of a School's Provision (Especially Teaching and Assessment) on Pupils' Standards, Achievement, Personal Development and Well-being in Physical Education

Purpose and Aims

This unit is about answering the questions, '**How well are we doing?**' and, '**How do we know how well we are doing?**' It will prepare leaders to make rigorous judgements about whether the quality of provision, especially the teaching, learning and assessment are good enough and are having a positive effect on learners' standards, achievement and well-being.

These judgements will be based on a range of evidence that includes observation of lessons, discussions with learners and analysis of written work.

Participants will practise applying the criteria rigorously and recording their findings. There will be a strong focus on inclusion in all activities to reflect the principles underpinning 'Every Child Matters'.

Participants will then evaluate their findings and practise writing the relevant section of the SEF, identifying strengths and areas for improvement to take forward into development planning.

Unit 3 Learning Outcomes

By the end of this unit, participants will be able to:

- accurately evaluate teaching, learning and assessment in terms of their impact on learners' achievement, personal development and well-being

- record judgements about teaching, learning and assessment clearly, accurately and unambiguously

- feed back their evaluation of teaching and learning to colleagues in a constructive and sensitive manner

- identify areas for improvement and plan related monitoring and evaluation activities.

Requirements

You will need:

- 'Every Child Matters: Framework for the Inspection of Schools in England' (Ofsted, 2005)

- a School Self-evaluation Form (SEF)

- 'High Quality Physical Education and Sport for Young People' (DfES, 2004)

- *A Guide to Self-review in Physical Education* (baalpe, 2006)

- *Achieving Excellence* (baalpe, 2004)

- QCA DVD materials or ACCAC video materials for National Curriculum Levels at KS 1, 2 and 3

- *Assessment for Learning in Physical Education* (baalpe, 2005)

- 'Inspecting Subjects 3–11: Physical Education' (pp 88–92), Appendix II (Ofsted, 2000)

- 'Inspecting Subjects 11–16: Physical Education with Guidance on Self-evaluation' (Ofsted, 2001)

- 'Inspecting Subjects Post–16: Physical Education with Guidance on Self-evaluation' (Ofsted, 2001).

Unit Development

3.1 Recognising High-quality Teaching and its Impact on Learners' Achievement in Physical Education and School Sport

    3.1.1 Questions raised in the SEF on teaching and learning

    3.1.2 Identifying characteristics of effective teaching

3.2 Identifying Key Sources of Evidence for Teaching and Learning

3.3 Observing, Evaluating and Recording High-quality Teaching and its Impact on Learners' Achievement, Personal Development and Well-being

    3.3.1 Using an evidence form to record observations and evaluations of a lesson

    3.3.2 Protocols for observing lessons

    3.3.3 Observing a lesson in your own school

3.4 Sharing Observations with Teachers

    3.4.1 Considerations when sharing observations with teachers

    3.4.2 Questions to ask when sharing lesson observations with teachers

    3.4.3 Observing feedback to teachers – using filmed material

3.5 Evaluating Findings and Writing a Report for the SEF

Table 4: Summary of tasks for Unit 3

Task 18 (10 minutes)	Identify the link between effective teaching and its impact on learners' outcomes.
Task 19 (20 minutes) Optional Task	Identify the characteristics of effective teaching to bring about HQPESS.
Task 20 (20 minutes)	Identify key sources of evidence on which to base evaluation of the quality of teaching and learning.
Task 21 (60 minutes)	Observe a filmed lesson.
Mid-course Task 22 (15 minutes)	Identify six elements that you feel should be included in the protocols for undertaking lesson observations.
Mid-course Task 23 (90 minutes)	Observe a lesson in your own school.
Mid-course Task 24 (15 minutes)	Considerations when sharing observations with teachers.
Mid-course Task 25 (20 minutes)	Observe the filmed feedback to teachers.
Optional Task 26 (30 minutes)	Role play and observation of feedback to teachers.
Mid-course Task 27 (90 minutes)	Give feedback on a lesson in your own setting.
Mid-course Task 28 (60 minutes)	Evaluate findings and write a section for the SEF on teaching and learning, including assessment.

3.1 Recognising High-quality Teaching and its Impact on Learners' Achievement in Physical Education and School Sport

3.1.1 Questions raised in the SEF on teaching and learning

5a. The School Self-evaluation Form, in Section 5a, asks how good is the quality of teaching and learning? The section looks to explore:

- how well teaching meets the needs of the full range of learners and how well it meets course requirements

- the suitability and rigour of assessment in planning learning and monitoring learners' progress

- the diagnosis of, and provision for, individual learning needs

- where appropriate, the involvement of parents and carers in their children's learning and development.

Teaching must be judged on its impact on the outcomes for learners.

5e. On the basis of your evaluation, what are your key priorities for development?

The outcomes for the learners in terms of their standards, progress and personal development and well-being form the primary evidence for the quality of teaching. Where, for example, the outcomes are good, the quality of teaching is likely to be good.

'Guidance for Inspectors of Schools: Conducting the Inspection' (Ofsted, July 2005).

Sometimes, only modest progress might be made, even when the teaching is very good, because of contextual factors such as schools facing really challenging circumstances.

3.1.2 Identifying characteristics of effective teaching

Task 18 (10 minutes)

This task deals with identifying the links between effective teaching and its impact on learners' outcomes.

Read and become familiar with the Ofsted evaluation schedule for the quality of teaching given below. Note the criteria in each judgement box relating to outcomes for learners (ie their achievement and personal development).

Table 5: Ofsted evaluation schedule for the quality of teaching

Outstanding (1)	Teaching is at least good in nearly all respects and is exemplary in significant elements. As a result, learners thrive and make exceptionally good progress.
Good (2)	Learners make good progress and show good attitudes to their work, as a result of effective teaching. The teachers' good subject knowledge lends confidence to their teaching styles, which engage learners and encourage them to work well independently. Any unsatisfactory behaviour is managed effectively. The level of challenge stretches without inhibiting. Based upon thorough and accurate assessment that informs learners how to improve, work is closely tailored to the full range of learners' needs, so that all can succeed. Learners are guided to assess their work themselves. Teaching assistants and other classroom helpers are well directed to support learning. Those with additional learning needs have work well matched to their needs, based upon a good diagnosis of them. Good relationships support parents/carers in helping learners to succeed.
Satisfactory (3)	Teaching is inadequate in no major respect and may be good in some respects, enabling learners to enjoy their education and make the progress that should be expected of them.
Inadequate (4)	Learners generally, or particular groups of them, do not make adequate progress in the subject because the teaching is unsatisfactory. Learners do not enjoy their work. Behaviour is often inappropriate. Teachers' knowledge of the subject or curriculum and the course requirements is inadequate, and the level of challenge is often wrongly pitched. The methods used do not sufficiently engage and encourage the learners. Not enough independent learning takes place, or learners are excessively passive. Inappropriate behaviour is not adequately managed. Assessment is not frequent or accurate enough to monitor learners' progress, so teachers do not have a clear enough understanding of learners' needs. Learners do not know how to improve. Teaching assistants, resources and parents/carers are inadequately utilised to support learners.

Taken from 'Guidance for the Inspection of Schools: Using the evaluation schedule' (Ofsted, 2005).

Characteristics of Effective Teaching

Teachers:

- have high expectations and engender a love of the subject

- have excellent subject knowledge of pedagogy

- assess learners regularly and rigorously, and use assessment data, including that from previous schools, to inform planning

- plan effectively for progression and continuity within the structure of the scheme of work

- ensure that they have clear learning objectives, which are shared with learners

- ensure that an appropriate range of strategies and materials are used to support learning for all learners

- use questioning and exposition effectively to establish links with prior learning and to develop and check current learning

- focus on developing core skills and ICT within the subject, alongside individual and collaborative study and problem-solving skills

- utilise opportunities to develop social, spiritual, moral and cultural awareness

- use a range of appropriate resources within lessons

- make effective use of time within lessons

- evaluate their teaching with a view to improvement

- share good practice with colleagues.

(The above section is taken from 'The National PESS Professional Development Programme Modules PD/Q and SD/Q: Evaluate to Inform and Improve' (DfES) Delegate Workbook, p14 and OHT 3.)

Inspiring Young People to Learn and Achieve in School

High-quality teachers and coaches:

- show commitment and enthusiasm

- provide positive role models

- show confidence in their learners' ability to make progress and achieve

- listen to their learners and value what they say and do

- raise their learners' aspirations and increase their determination to make progress and succeed

- have pride in and celebrate their learners' successes

- let pupils' parents/carers know what they have learnt and achieved in PE and school sport

- improve their own subject expertise.

[handwritten note:] ICT can help here too.

[handwritten note:] important correlates with assessment, teacher feeding back what they have achieved & what they have not. ICT can assist.

Helping Young People to Learn and Achieve in School

To make a positive impact on pupils' learning and achievement, high-quality teachers and coaches need to:

- have a clear plan that sets out steps towards meeting the school's vision and expectations for PE and school sport

- share with learners what they expect them to achieve, in a way that they can understand

- take into account what learners have already learnt within and beyond school

- identify the next steps in progression and communicate these to learners and their parents/carers

- give each learner relevant learning activities and authentic contexts that interest, excite and motivate them

- provide opportunities for learners to analyse, assess and evaluate their own and others' work

- give learners time to think, reflect and make decisions for themselves

- allow learners time to wrestle with problems, while giving well-timed advice and support to advance learning and avoid frustration.

(The above section is taken from 'High Quality Physical Education and Sport for Young People' (DfES, 2005) pp 16–17.)

Further reading:

- *A Guide to Self-review in Physical Education* (baalpe, 2006).

- Appendix II in 'Inspecting Subjects 3–11: Physical Education' (Ofsted, 2000) pp 88 –92.

- 'Inspecting Subjects 11–16: Physical Education with Guidance on Self-evaluation' (Ofsted, 2001).

- 'Inspecting Subjects Post-16: Physical Education with Guidance on Self-evaluation' (Ofsted, 2001).

For further exemplification of learner outcomes, see the DfES booklet 'High Quality Physical Education and Sport in Your School' ('HQPESS') (2004).

Task 19 (20 minutes) – Optional

This task deals with identifying the characteristics of effective teaching to bring about HQPESS.

Work on your own or with a colleague(s).

- Create a set of criteria for effective teaching that are needed to ensure HQPESS using the Ofsted criteria for teaching and the criteria given above.

- Give examples of good practice found in your own setting.

- How does your list compare with the list given in the 'National PESS Professional Development Programme Modules PD/Q and SD/Q: Evaluate to Inform and Improve' delegate workbook?

HQPESS outcomes	Criteria for effective teaching	Examples of good practice in my school
Young people:		
1. are committed		
2. know and understand what they are trying to achieve		
3. understand that PE and sport form part of a healthy, active lifestyle		
4. have the confidence to get involved in PE and sport		
5. have the skill and control that they need to take part in PE and sport		

6. willingly take part in a range of competitive, creative and challenge-type activities		
7. think about and make appropriate decisions for themselves		
8. show a desire to improve and achieve in relation to their own abilities		
9. have the stamina, suppleness and strength to keep going		
10. enjoy PE, school and community sport.		

Use this box to highlight any areas you know you need to do more work on or improve, then transfer this to your SEF and action plan (see Task 28, Unit 3 and Task 33, Unit 4):

3.2 Identifying Key Sources of Evidence for Teaching and Learning

Where do you find the evidence to help evaluate the quality of teaching and learning? The following task helps you to consider where and how to collect the evidence to enable an accurate judgement on the quality of teaching and learning.

Remember it is the **impact on pupils' learning, progress, achievement and standards** that is the main criteria against which to evaluate the quality of teaching.

Task 20 (20 minutes)

Working on your own or with a colleague(s):

- identify the key sources of evidence on which to base evaluations of the quality of teaching and learning
- identify where you have gathered evidence and evaluated it – what did it tell you?
- identify where you need to spend more time gathering evidence and evaluating it.

Key sources of evidence for the quality of teaching and learning	Identify where you have gathered evidence and evaluated it – what did it tell you? (ie areas of strength and areas for improvement)	Do you need to spend more time gathering this type of evidence?

Key sources of evidence for evaluating teaching and learning:

- Lessons
- Learners' written work
- Results and assessments
- Discussions with learners
- Observation of extra-curricular activities
- Observation of coaches and adults other than teachers (AOTTs).

3.3 Observing, Evaluating and Recording High-quality Teaching and its Impact on Learners' Achievement, Personal Development and Well-being

Participants will use filmed lessons from the case study schools.

3.3.1 Using an evidence form to record observations and evaluations of a lesson

In order to come to an overall evaluation of the lesson, see the Ofsted guidance below on where to pitch judgements.

Table 6: Guidance on where to pitch judgements about the overall quality of a lesson

Description	Characteristics of the Lesson
Outstanding (1)	The lesson is at least good in all or nearly all respects and is exemplary in significant elements, as shown by the exceptional enjoyment and progress of the learners.
Good (2)	Most learners make good progress because of the good teaching they receive. Behaviour overall is good and learners are keen to get on with their work in a secure and friendly environment in which they can thrive. The health and safety of the learners is not endangered. Teaching is well informed, confident, engaging and precise. The work is well matched to the full range of learners' needs, so that most are suitably challenged. Teaching methods are effectively related to the lesson's objectives and the needs of learners. Teaching assistants and resources are well deployed and good use is made of time. Assessment of learners' work is regular and consistent, and makes a good contribution to their progress.
Satisfactory (3)	The lesson is inadequate in no major respect, and may be good in some respects, as shown by the satisfactory enjoyment and progress of learners.

Inadequate (4)	A lesson cannot be adequate if:
	• most learners, or a significant specific minority of learners, make less-than-satisfactory progress, whether this is due to unsatisfactory teaching or the impact of bad behaviour
	• learners' overall behaviour or attitudes are unsatisfactory and the tone of the lesson is inimical to the development of learners' personal qualities
	• the health and safety of learners is endangered
	• the teaching is unsatisfactory – this will usually cause the learners' progress to be unsatisfactory but, occasionally, progress will be satisfactory in spite of the teaching, due to the good attitudes of the learners.
	Unsatisfactory teaching is likely to display one or more of the following points:
	• Weak knowledge of the curriculum leading to inaccurate teaching and low demands of pupils.
	• Work badly matched to pupils' starting points.
	• Ineffective classroom management of behaviour.
	• Methods which are poorly geared to the learning objectives or which fail to gain the interest or commitment of the learners.
	• Inadequate use of resources, including assistants and the time available.
	• Poor assessment.

'Guidance on the Use of Evidence Forms' ref: HMI 2505 (Ofsted, July 2005)

Also refer to 'Evidence Form and Grade Criteria for Lessons' in *A Guide to Self-review in Physical Education* (baalpe, 2006).

Note the differences in the Ofsted guidance for judging the **quality of a lesson**, given above, as compared to the guidance for judging the **quality of teaching overall**, given at the start of the unit. The emphasis throughout is on the **impact** of the teaching on learners' progress.

The overall judgement of a lesson will be the 'best fit' of the grade descriptions in the box, except in the case of an unsatisfactory lesson, where particular conditions mean that the lesson cannot be satisfactory.

The Ofsted evidence form (EF) on the next page is provided for recording observations and evaluations of lessons. It includes guidance on what to look for and can be used as a prompt sheet for observers. Beware of being restricted by adherence to personal preferred teaching approaches.

Evidence Form										
Inspector's OIN:		Inspection number:			Observation time:			Observation type:		L A D O
Year group(s):		Grouping:	MC SU SA SL O			BO GI MI		Present/N OR:		
Subject codes:			Support teachers/ assistants	SEN T S	EAL T S	Oth T S		Inspector's EF No:		

Focus: (ie main purpose of the inspection activity):

The focus should arise from the subject's priorities for improvement. The focus could usefully be posed as a question to be answered and then be referred to throughout the EF.

Context:

Include learning objectives.
Details of groups of learners – SEN/ENG/EAL/gender/ability.
Prior experience or attainment.
Number of lesson in the series or unit.

Evaluation:

How well are learners making progress and benefiting in terms of their personal development? Look at: rates of learning; ways in which they learn; enjoyment; participation; behaviour; attitudes.
(HQPESS outcomes – commitment, enjoyment and desire to improve (1, 8 and 10), understanding and thinking (2, 5 and 7), fitness and a healthy, active lifestyle (3 and 9), confidence to take part (4 and 6) and skills (5).

*What is **helping** learners to learn, make progress and enjoy the lesson?*
(Challenge; pace; variety of activity; activities matched to individuals; knowledge of what they are aiming to achieve and how well they are doing; relationships.)

*What is **holding the learners back** from learning and making progress as well as they can?*
*How well do learners **make progress** in all four aspects of the NC, basic skills and ICT?*
*Are there any **differences** between groups of learners?*

Summary of main points:

Major strengths and areas for improvement (ie what really aids learning, progress and personal development, and what holds it back).
Answer the focus questions.

Judgement on the overall quality of the lesson (Leave blank when not a lesson): 1 = Outstanding, 4 = Inadequate	

Use for grades if there is sufficient evidence:

Standards (Leave blank when observing single lessons)	Progress	Personal development	Teaching	Curriculum	Care, guidance and support	Leadership and management

Particular evaluations related to safety, health, enjoyment, contribution to the community and economic well-being:

Outcomes observed that relate to the five areas of 'Every Child Matters'.
Features of the provision that contribute to the five areas of 'Every Child Matters' criteria.

Different Approaches to Recording Evidence

You may wish to consider the different approaches to recording the evidence on the forms in the case study material. There is no right or wrong way of how you set out the evidence form. You may wish to use markers such as plus (+) and minus (-) signs for positive and negative points, or columns to identify strengths and weaknesses. However, there are important generic characteristics of a well-written evidence form (EF) – see below.

The Characteristics of a Well-written Evidence Form

• An appropriate balance of evaluation and description, with greater weight given to the former.

• A clear evaluation of the effect of teaching and learning on learners' standards, and achievement and personal development.

• Clear reference to the focus of the evaluation throughout the EF.

• A flavour of the subject being observed.

• Grades that reflect the text and the balance of strengths and weaknesses.

• Clarity of information about the context and content of the lesson.

Task 21 (60 minutes)

This task deals with observation of a filmed lesson.

Working on your own or with a colleague(s):

• use the filmed material and choose a lesson (Primary – Year 2 Basic Skills or Year 6 Gymnastics; Secondary – Year 7 Athletics or Year 10 GCSE theory)

• observe the description of the school outlined by the head teacher and the description of the lesson and class given by the teachers for each lesson, in order to complete the context of the lesson and the focus of the observation

• refer to case study material in Appendices I and II

• observe the lesson and complete the EF on the next page or download one from the Ofsted website (www.ofsted.gov.uk), using the Ofsted criteria to help make evaluations.

Sample evidence form

Evidence Form												

Inspector's OIN:		Inspection number:			Observation time:			Observation type:		L A D O	

Year group(s):		Grouping:	MC SU SA SL O		BO GI MI		Present/NOR:	

Subject codes:			Support teachers/ assistants:	SEN	T	S	EAL	T	S	Oth	T	S	Inspector's EF No:	

Focus: (ie main purpose of the inspection activity)

Context:

Evaluation:

Summary of main points:

Judgement on the overall quality of the lesson (Leave blank when not a lesson): 1 = Outstanding, 4 = Inadequate

Use for grades if there is sufficient evidence:

Standards	Progress	Personal development	Teaching	Curriculum	Care, guidance and support	Leadership and management

Particular evaluations related to safety, health, enjoyment, contribution to the community and economic well-being:

Visit www.ofsted.gov.uk to download your own form. (Document reference number: HMI2506 [July 2005.])

3.3.2 Protocols for observing lessons

Whatever the scope and focus of lesson observations, a code of conduct should be established and followed by all involved.

Mid-course Task 22 (15 minutes)

Working on your own or with a colleague(s), identify six elements that you feel should be included in the protocols for undertaking lesson observations.

Suggested Protocols for Observing Lessons
1.
2.
3.
4.
5.
6.

Protocols for observing lessons should include the following principles:

- Communication with staff should be purposeful and productive.

- Evaluations of lessons should be objective and impartial, and be presented honestly, clearly and frankly, ensuring that judgements are accurate and reliable.

- All staff should be treated with courtesy, respect and sensitivity.

- Teachers' confidence should be built up and mutual respect established.

- All efforts should be made to minimise the stress on teachers being observed.

- Observers should ensure that they understand what a teacher is doing and why.

- Findings on lessons observed should be shared with teachers in a helpful way.

- Confidentiality of information should be respected – especially regarding evaluations made on individual teachers.

- A teacher's work should not be discussed within earshot of others.

- Concerns that need to be discussed with senior managers or the head teacher should be discussed with the teacher concerned beforehand.

3.3.3 Observing a lesson in your own school

Lesson Observation – Protocols

The selection of lessons to be observed and the focus for the lesson observations should arise from current priorities for improvement.

Though leaders will often observe lessons, peer evaluation should be encouraged.

Fitness for purpose should be clearly understood:

- Why is the lesson being observed?

- Has the purpose been agreed with the teacher?

- Why has this particular lesson been selected?

- What is the focus of the lesson observation?

Procedures should be clear and understood by the evaluator and the teacher:

- Reading/collecting 'evidence' in advance of, and during, the lesson is essential.
  For example:
  – What are the objectives for teaching and learning?
  – How will you assess the extent to which these have been achieved?

- The role of the observer, their place in the room and their contribution (or not) to the lesson must be agreed.

- The pro forma to be used must be agreed.

- 'Evidence' for the lesson must be identified (eg lesson plan, place of lesson in module/scheme).
- The nature of the teaching group, the use of resources and the non-teaching staff available must be identified.
- Courtesies must be observed (eg thanks to the teacher, learners).
- The time and venue for feedback must be agreed and understood.
- The audience for outcomes/dissemination must be clear and understood.
- Feedback must be verbal and written.
- Copies of feedback to other colleagues must be agreed beforehand (eg staff-development tutor).

Conduct of the observer in a lesson:

- Be unobtrusive.
- Talk to learners about their work, but not in a way that disrupts the lesson or their learning.
- Avoid approaching the teacher during the course of the lesson.
- Ensure that you observe the different ability groups within the class.
- Avoid making contributions to the lesson, unless pre-arranged with the teacher.

Mid-course Task 23 (90 minutes)

This task deals with observing a lesson in your own school.

Working on your own:

- observe the lesson
- complete the EF on the next page or download one from the Ofsted website (www.ofsted.gov.uk), using the Ofsted criteria to help make evaluations.

Sample evidence form

Evidence Form									
Inspector's OIN:		Inspection number:			Observation time:			Observation type:	L A D O
Year group(s):		Grouping:		MC SU SA SL O		BO GI MI		Present/NOR:	
Subject codes:			Support teachers/ assistants:	SEN	T	S	EAL	T	S	Oth	T	S	Inspector's EF No:	

Focus: (ie main purpose of the inspection activity)

Context:

Evaluation:

Summary of main points:

Judgement on the overall quality of the lesson (Leave blank when not a lesson):   1 = Outstanding, 4 =

Use for grades if there is sufficient evidence:

Standards	Progress	Personal development	Teaching	Curriculum	Care, guidance and support	Leadership and management

Particular evaluations related to safety, health, enjoyment, contribution to the community and economic well-being:

Visit www.ofsted.gov.uk to download your own form. (Document reference number: HMI2506 [July 2005.])

3.4 Sharing Observations with Teachers

3.4.1 Considerations when sharing observations with teachers

Mid-course Task 24 (15 minutes)

Work on your own:

• List what you think are the main considerations when sharing observations with teachers.

• Compare these with the list provided below.

Considerations when sharing observations with teachers:

Comparisons with those listed:

When sharing observations with teachers, there are a number of significant points that need remembering:

• A relaxed but professional atmosphere should be established quickly.

• Focus should be on the impact of the teaching on learners' achievement and personal development.

• Judgements should be clear and accurate.

• Judgements must be fair and backed with evidence. Remember: it is not your lesson. Comments such as, 'I wouldn't have done that' or, 'I would have possibly…' are inappropriate and can be counterproductive.

• Evaluations should recognise strengths as well as weaknesses.

• The focus should be on the act, not the person.

• Opportunities for discussion should be given.

• You should avoid overwhelming the teacher with too many weaknesses.

• You should give helpful advice that will lead to action.

• You should acknowledge improvements as soon as possible after the initial observation.

• You should work to the protocol and code of conduct.

3.4.2 Types of Questions to Ask when Sharing Lesson Observations with Teachers

Open Questions

Open questions are designed to elicit as much information as possible. For example:

• Which part of your teaching do you enjoy most?

• How would you describe your experience of…?

• What would you want to gain from this course?

• What do you think would be the best way to take this forward?

Probing Questions

These are designed to go deeper into the issue, in order to gain quality information. For example:

• In what way?

• How did you feel when you had completed that work?

• What makes that part of the job interesting/more satisfying/difficult?

• Will you expand on that a little?

• Why is that important?

• What makes it helpful/difficult to work in that way?

Reflective Questions

These are questions that check out understanding and reflect information back to the teacher in order for him/her to develop the issue further. For example:

• So are you saying that…?

• Are you telling me that…?

• If I were to summarise what you've said, would I be right in saying…?

Closed Questions

These can be used to gather information or to check facts. For example:

• Have you used this computer program often?

• What resources do you use for...?

• Where did you find this information?

Closed questions lead to specific information or the reply 'yes' or 'no'. They may need to be followed up with more open questions. For example:

• Have you used this reading text before? (*closed*)

• What did you think of it? (*open*)

• What are the advantages of using this one? (*open*)

• Are there any disadvantages? (*closed*)

• How did you overcome these? (*open*)

Multiple Questions

These are when two or more questions are asked at the same time. For example:

• Will you tell me what you've done best and what you'd like to improve on?

• Are you happy with the agenda? Would you like to add something or do you think we should approach it differently?

They are best avoided, as they are often confusing. Usually, only one question will be answered.

Leading Questions

These can be frustrating if used too often or inappropriately, but they can sometimes be useful for exerting influence. For example:

• I'm sure you can see the advantages of this, can't you?

• Don't you think that would be a good idea?

You are likely to get a positive response whether the teacher agrees with you or not. It is important to follow up with an open question. For example:

• I'm sure you can see the advantages of this, can't you? (*leading*)

• What are the advantages? (*open*)

3.4.3 Observing feedback to teachers – using filmed material

Task 25 Observing the filmed feedback to teachers (20 minutes)

Working on your own:

• select from the DVD the feedback session relevant to the lesson you have observed. Use the prompts below to evaluate the quality of the feedback and identify strengths and areas for improvement using the aide-memoire

• compare your evaluation of the feedback to the notes in Appendices I and II.

Points to Observe	Notes
How sensitively are the messages being delivered (eg tone, body language, eye contact)?	
Do the messages come across clearly, constructively and in a way that is helpful to the teacher?	
Are strengths recognised and encouraged as well as weaknesses emphasised? Is the balance about right?	
Are difficult messages delivered clearly, unambiguously, sensitively and confidently?	
Is it a dialogue? Is the teacher involved in the process through his/her own evaluation?	
Are both the observer and the teacher involved in discussing the best ways to improve practice?	
Is the feedback based on sufficient evidence that has both description and evaluation?	
Does the observer respond appropriately to questions, comments etc from the teacher?	
Is the teacher ready to receive the feedback?	

Overall, does the feedback give the teacher a clear indication of his or her strengths and a clear target for improvement and development? Is there agreement on this?

Task 26 Role play and observing of feedback to teachers (30 minutes) – Optional

Use the lesson observed in Task 21, or view another lesson from the DVD and write notes on it on the evidence form.

In threes, role play the feedback session for the lesson you have just observed:

1. Teacher – identify the major issues for your feedback and refer to the quality prompts.
2. Mentor – note how you feel while being given the feedback.
3. Observer – use the prompts to evaluate the quality of the feedback.

Compare your feedback on the DVD to the notes in Appendices I and II.

Task 27 Giving feedback on a lesson in your own setting (90 minutes)

This task deals with giving feedback on a lesson in your own setting.

Following agreement and using the protocols highlighted, carry out one or more lesson observations in your own school. Use the evidence form to record the information and feed back to the person observed. See if you can arrange for your mentor to observe the feedback and evaluate it using the proforma on page 88.

3.5 Evaluating Findings and Writing a Report for the SEF

You need to complete a SEF for your subject. To remind yourself of the criteria for writing a good SEF, see Unit 1.

Criteria for a Good SEF

Your SEF should:

• convey a clear picture of how well the subject/school is doing

• provide proof of how you know what you know

• show what you are doing to build on successes and to remedy weaknesses.

You should look for:

• clear judgements based on the framework criteria

• judgements that are supported by a good range of key evidence

• clear identification of strengths, weaknesses and priorities for improvement

• links between issues raised in the Achievement section and how the school is tackling these in the sections on Provision and Leadership and Management.

Look at the special school and the secondary school examples of completed sections of the SEF on Achievement and Standards and Personal Development in Unit 1.

Look at the example of a completed secondary school SEF in Appendix III.

Task 28 Evaluate findings and write a section for the SEF on teaching and learning, including assessment (60 minutes)

Working on your own or with a colleague(s), evaluate your findings and write a section for the SEF on Teaching and Learning, including Assessment.

Refer back to notes you have made in Table 2 in Unit 1.

Unit 4: Evaluating Leadership and Management

Purpose and Aims

This unit helps participants to understand what is meant by effective leadership and effective management. Participants will identify key sources of evidence on which evaluations can be made.

It also brings together all their findings and helps participants to identify what needs to happen next to plan action for improvement. Unless action follows, there is no point in self-evaluation. Nothing ever grows solely through measuring it. At this point, participants should have made judgements about learners' standards, achievement, personal development and well-being, teaching and learning based on the analysis of evidence from across a range of sources. They will have identified strengths and areas for improvement.

Participants will draw up an action plan based on an intelligent analysis of the findings of their self-evaluation activities.

They will draw up a succinct and accurate report to contribute to the school's self-evaluation form (SEF). They will consider how to best monitor and evaluate the plans they make and so develop a realistic, cyclical programme of self-evaluation activity that will sustain improvements.

Unit 4 Learning Outcomes

By the end of this unit, participants will be able to:

- recognise effective leadership and management and key sources of evidence
- evaluate the findings of monitoring activities, applying HQPESS and Ofsted criteria rigorously
- draw up a plan for improvement, identifying manageable self-evaluation activity
- produce information that will contribute to the whole school self-evaluation process
- plan a programme of effective self-evaluation.

Requirements

You will need:

- 'Every Child Matters: Framework for the Inspection of Schools in England from September 2005' (Ofsted, 2005)
- a School Self-evaluation Form (SEF) from the Ofsted website
- 'High Quality PE and Sport for Young People' (DfES, 2004)
- *A Guide to Self-review in Physical Education* (baalpe, 2006)
- *Achieving Excellence: Subject Leadership in Physical Education* (baalpe, 2004)
- Modules SD/Q and PD/Q – Evaluate to Inform and Improve, from the National PESS Professional Development Programme – DfES, 2005
- 'Do you Have High Quality PE and Sport in your School?' (DfES, 2005)
- your own subject improvement plan
- access to the QCA PESS website (www.qca.org.uk/pess).

Unit Development

4.1 What is Effective Leadership and Management?

    4.1.1 Questions raised in the SEF on leadership and management

    4.1.2 Checklist for effective leadership and management

    4.1.3 Identifying key sources of evidence

    4.1.4 Examples of effective leadership and management

4.2 Evaluating Findings and Writing a Report for the Self-evaluation Form

    4.2.1 Evaluating findings and writing a report for the SEF

    4.2.2 Contributing to your own school's SEF

4.3 Identifying the Key Components of a Good-quality Action Plan

4.4 Drawing up an Improvement/Development/Action Plan Based on the Priorities Identified in Table 2 Unit 1

4.5 Recap of the Self-evaluation and School Improvement Processes

4.6 What Next? Personal Target Setting – Short, Medium and Long Term

Table 7: Summary of Tasks for Unit 4

	Mid-course Task 29 (15 minutes)	From your own experience, draw up a set of criteria relating to good leadership and effective management.
	Mid-course Task 30 (10 minutes)	Audit features of effective leadership and management in your own setting.
	Post-course Task 31 (30 minutes)	Contribute to your own school's SEF.
	Mid-course Task 32 (30 minutes)	Form a critical analysis of a subject/department's action plan.
	Post-course Task 33 (45 minutes)	Draw up an improvement/development plan based on two of the priorities you have identified. Include a plan for self-evaluation of activity to fit in with the school's cycle of planning.
	Task 34 (15 minutes)	What next? Getting started.

4.1 What is Effective Leadership and Management?

The hallmark of good leadership and management lies in their impact on the quality of provision, especially teaching, and the standards achieved by learners within the subject. How do curriculum leaders assure the quality of that for which they are responsible? For example, do they have a well-founded view of what amounts to good teaching?

When judging your provision for leadership and management, it is important to link them to outcomes. If the learners are doing well, how does the provision and leadership and management facilitate their achievement?

Ofsted Direct, Issue 4, Autumn term 2005/06.

The SEF in Section 6 indicates that 'your evaluation of leadership and management should take account of their impact in terms of the outcomes for learners and the quality of provision' (SEF).

4.1.1 Questions raised in the SEF on leadership and management

The Self-evaluation Form (SEF) in Section 6 on leadership and management asks the questions:

6a.   What is the overall effectiveness and efficiency of leadership and management?

• How effectively leaders and managers at all levels set **clear direction** leading to improvement and promote high-quality integrated care and education.

• How effectively performance is **monitored and improved** to meet challenging targets through high-quality assurance and self-assessment.

• How well equality of opportunity is promoted and discrimination tackled, so that all learners achieve their potential (ie inclusion).

• The adequacy and suitability of staff, specialist equipment, learning resources and accommodation.

• How effectively and efficiently resources are deployed to achieve value for money.

• How effectively links are made with other providers, services, employers and organisations to promote the integration of care, education and extended services to enhance learning.

• The extent to which governors (and, if appropriate, other supervisory boards) discharge their responsibilities.

6b.   Where relevant, the effectiveness and efficiency of leadership and management in the sixth form.

6c.   On the basis of your evaluation, what are your key priorities for development?

To make judgements, refer to the judgement columns in the tables in *A Guide to Self-review in Physical Education* (baalpe, 2006).

Mid-course Task 29 (15 minutes)

From your own experience, draw up a set of criteria relating to good leadership and effective management.

When complete, compare with the checklist given below.

Self-study: work on your own or with a colleague(s).
Taught course: work on your own, then share and discuss findings with the group as a whole (15 minutes).

Criteria for Good Leadership	Criteria for Effective Management

4.1.2 Checklist for effective leadership and management

Within a wider context, the process identified in 'High Quality PE and Sport for Young People' relating to high-quality leadership and management is about creating the vision and making the vision reality.

'When creating the vision, high-quality school leaders will:

- recognise what PE and school sport can achieve for each learner and the whole school

- set high expectations of what individual learners can achieve in and through PE and school sport

- explain the value of PE and school sport to learning, health and well-being in a way that learners, teachers, parents and governors can understand.

When making the vision reality, high-quality school leaders and managers:

- are creative and strategic in providing enough time, teachers and coaches, space and equipment to enable learners to learn and achieve

- support and develop teachers and coaches to enable learners to achieve more

- use the information from monitoring and evaluating the impact of PE and school sport to ensure the school's vision is met

- listen to learners and act on what they say

- celebrate learners' achievements, so they feel successful and valued

- involve and inform parents/carers and listen to and act on what they say.'

'High Quality PE and Sport for Young People', pp 14–17 (DfES, 2004).

Criteria for effective leadership

- Clear vision for the direction and development of the subject, focused on high-quality outcomes for every learner.

- Clear focus on inclusion.

- Vision articulated to staff with enthusiasm and a strong commitment to fulfilling the vision.

- Wide-ranging, up-to-date knowledge of national and local strategies and an understanding of these on the work of the subject.

- Innovative leader with a strategic view.

- Clear direction from the leader, who sets high standards.

- Staff inspired by the leader and wanting to follow their lead, confident in their knowledge and ability.

- Staff knowing what is expected of them (job profiles) and work effectively delegated with appropriate support.

- The leader as a model of good practice in relation to teaching.

- Good communication across the team.

- Teamwork being actively promoted.

Criteria for effective management

- Systematic and rigorous monitoring and evaluation of the work of the subject.

- Clearly identified priorities.

- Action to improve being planned succinctly, with success criteria related to learners' outcomes identified.

- Well-planned teaching and learning across the subject.

- Plans to ensure equality of opportunity for all learners.

- Good day-to-day organisation to ensure smooth running of the subject.

- Good management of resources to enhance learners' achievement.

- Resulting value for money.

For specific criteria relating to leadership and management in the Ofsted framework, see pages 12–14 in the overview and also *A Guide to Self-review in Physical Education* (baalpe, 2006). Further guidance is also available in *Achieving Excellence* and *Subject Leadership in Physical Education* (baalpe, 2004).

Mid-course Task 30 (10 minutes)

This task deals with an audit of the features of effective leadership and management in your own setting.

Work on your own or with a colleague(s).

Using the criteria given on the previous pages, indicate the present position of these aspects within your school. Use different coloured highlighters to indicate 'met', 'working towards' and 'need to work on'.

Then fill in the box below.

Choose one strength in leadership within your school and indicate what impact it has on learners' outcomes:
Choose one strength in management within your school and indicate what impact it has on learners' outcomes:
Indicate one area for improvement in management within your school to be followed up in the action plan:

4.1.3 Identifying key sources of evidence

You must identify the impact of actions related to leadership and management on the outcomes for pupils. However, it is useful to look for key sources of evidence related to leadership and management. Use the model below to aid your evaluation.

Key sources of evidence and questions to consider when evaluating the impact of leadership and management are identified in the following table.

Table 8: Model of auditing leadership and management

Evidence	Questions to Ask of the Evidence	Yes	No	Partly
Subject improvement plan (SIP)	• Does the SIP identify how the standards and achievement of learners will be improved? • Does the SIP identify how the standards and achievement of any groups of learners will be improved? • Are the targets set for improvement in achievement and standards specific and measurable? • Are there specific, measurable, time-related and resourced success criteria in place? • Are arrangements for monitoring the action in place? • Are arrangements for evaluating the success of the action in place? • Are the persons responsible for monitoring and evaluating the success of the action identified? • Are time targets made clear?			
Self-evaluation: a. Pupil performance data analysis b. Lesson monitoring records c. Work scrutiny monitoring records d. Records of discussions with pupils, parents, staff and other stakeholders e. Other monitoring records	• Does analysis of performance data identify strengths and areas for improvement across the NC/parts of the course? • Does it identify underperformance of any groups of pupils? • Are the monitoring of lessons and of work scrutiny focused on the impact of teaching on pupils' learning and progress? • Are discussions with pupils, parents, staff and stakeholders well focused?			

Table 8: Model of auditing leadership and management (continued)

Evidence	Questions to Ask of the Evidence	Yes	No	Partly
Professional-development arrangements	• Do all staff, including non-teaching staff, have the opportunity for INSET? • Is professional development focused on the school and subject priorities? • Is best practice in T and L identified within the subject and shared on a regular basis?			
Performance-management arrangements Job descriptions	• Do staff have PM targets that are linked to school/subject priorities for improvement? • Do job descriptions outline responsibilities and accountability for standards and quality of provision?			
Subject policies: a. Teaching and learning b. Assessment c. Homework d. Routines and procedures e. Health and safety f. Risk assessments g. Out-of-school-hours learning policy	• Have all staff contributed to subject policies? • Are there monitoring arrangements in place to check that policies are carried out across the subject? • Is risk assessment in place for all activities and working areas?			
Curriculum plan Schemes of work Lesson planning	• Do all learners receive their full National Curriculum entitlement? • Do all teachers follow the schemes of work and curriculum plan? • How often are curriculum plans and schemes of work reviewed? • Are lesson plans monitored and do teachers review their impact on learners' progress? • Does the review take full account of their effect on learners' progress?			

4.1.4 Examples of effective leadership and management

> **Example of Good Leadership and Management**
>
> *The school sports coordinator worked effectively in partnership with subject leaders across a number of schools in the Barrow-in-Furness area, building on their commitment, enthusiasm and vision for high-quality physical education and school sport.*
>
> *The subject leaders carried out an audit of provision of physical education and school sport in the schools. This included interviewing staff and pupils, observing playground activities and analysing participation in lessons and out-of-school-hours learning. From these, priorities for improvement were identified and an improvement plan was drawn up. Good leadership ensured that there was a high level of commitment to the action needed to make improvements across the partnership. Good management ensured that plans set out clear action to take and that the impact of the action was evaluated.*
>
> *The work of the Cumbria Partnership based in Barrow-in-Furness, comprising three primary schools, one special school and six secondary schools, focused on improving learners' attitudes to learning and leadership skills. To achieve these objectives, the schools – in partnership – used the following strategies. They:*
> * *used young leaders and mentors*
> * *set up festivals*
> * *organised playgrounds*
> * *trained midday supervisors*
> * *provided new resources for playground activities*
> * *reorganised learner groups in the curriculum, including using single-gender groupings*
> * *introduced the Junior Sports Leader Award*
> * *changed activities in PE lessons and after school in response to feedback from learners.*
>
> *The outcomes were positive, with learners' attitudes to PE and school sport changing significantly – especially in the secondary schools, where girls' attendance and participation in lessons rose considerably. The number of learners taking part in after-school sport rose across the partnership. In the primary and special schools, positive play at lunchtimes increased, and learners were more ready to settle down in afternoon classes. The self-esteem of learners acting as leaders grew. Relationships between younger and older learners became more positive.'*
>
> Example from 'The National PESS Professional Development Programme Modules SD/Q and PD/Q'

4.2 Evaluating Findings and Writing a Report for the Self-evaluation Form

4.2.1 Evaluating findings and writing a report for the SEF

Having audited leadership and management activities and considered their impact on learners' standards and achievement and on the quality of provision (section 4.1.3), you are now in a position to draw up the section in the SEF on leadership and management.

Revisit the examples of SEFs and your analysis of sections of them (Unit 1). Remind yourself of the criteria for a well-written SEF (Unit 1). Remember, there is no right or wrong way to set out a SEF, but it needs to be helpful to the subject leaders, school leaders and governors in identifying not only strengths, but the priorities for the subject.

The results of your evaluation using the high-quality learner outcomes should form the basis for deciding your priorities for change.

Your priorities may relate to specific groups of pupils. For example, you may decide to concentrate your efforts on:
- *increasing the proportion of pupils who consistently meet most of the outcomes well*
- *reducing the proportion of pupils who demonstrate only a few of the outcomes.*

You may decide to focus on a specific group of outcomes or just one outcome. For example:
- *improving pupils' attitudes to PESS (their commitment, confidence, desire to improve and enjoyment)*
- *increasing the consistency with which some pupils demonstrate that they have the skills and control that they need to take part in PESS.*

There is no right or wrong order to tackle different areas for improvement. What you identify as your priority will depend on the particular needs that you have found evidence of through your self-evaluation. You may find that tackling one area as a priority will automatically bring about improvements in another. For example, increasing the number of pupils who are demonstrating all of the outcomes of high-quality PESS may mean that the number of pupils demonstrating fewer than half of the high-quality outcomes will diminish.

'Do you Have High Quality PE and Sport in your School?' (DfES, 2005).

4.2.2 Contributing to your own school's SEF

Post-course Task 31 (30 minutes)

Working on your own or with a colleague(s):
- analyse leadership and management and its impact on learners' outcomes – refer to the questions in section 4.1.1
- write a summary of the strengths, weaknesses and priorities for improvement, giving a clear indication of the sources of evidence.

Summary of strengths and weaknesses, with reference to sources of evidence:

Priorities for improvement:

4.3 Identifying the Key Components of a Good-quality Action Plan

Effective subject action/development/improvement plans are a key indicator of the way a department or subject is led and managed. They should promote high standards and effective teaching and learning. They should be based upon an audit of strengths, weaknesses and needs as identified through self-evaluation activity and set out in the SEF. Their purpose is to identify the vision and aims of the subject, taking account of appropriate national strategies and setting a rationale for priorities. They should be clearly focused on raising standards and achievement, and improving the quality of teaching and learning.

The action plan should embrace the following key components or **SMART targets**:

- **S**pecific – concise goals that are measurable in terms of qualitative and quantitative criteria for success which specify outcomes/standards and the effects/impact on learners.

- **M**anageable – a manageable selection of innovations that will help the department/subject move forward and raise standards (a maximum of 3–5 over two or three years).

- **A**chievable – realistic targets that are possible, with appropriate steps/tasks identified that will achieve the target.

- **R**esourced – an identification of additional resources needed to support/lead development (eg human resources, equipment/materials, CPD, budget costs).

- **T**ime-related – an indication of timescales and completion dates.

The plan should also include:

- processes for monitoring and regular review and evaluation of progress, identifying the persons responsible

- a focus on staff development and training

- links to performance management.

Now that we have highlighted the possible contents of a plan, the following series of questions can be utilised to quality-assure the content and processes involved in implementation:

- Does the physical education department plan:
  - identify appropriate priorities and targets?
  - take the necessary action?
  - review its progress towards them?
  - provide information relevant to the completion of the School Improvement Plan and the SEF?

- Are the department/subject priorities and targets appropriate?
  - Do they link to priorities stipulated by the school?
  - Are the tasks to be undertaken clear?
  - Are they appropriate to any self-review, LA review, National Strategy review or Inspection that has been undertaken recently?
  - Are any post-review/post-inspection action points addressed clearly?
  - Are there clear programmes of action and is allocation of resources, time and staff linked to priorities?
  - Is there a clear allocation of responsibilities, with appropriate division of responsibilities between evaluation and monitoring?
  - Does each target have success criteria, coastings and deadlines?
  - Do criteria for judging success vary in clarity and usefulness for evaluation?

– Are some criteria vague and general, others precise and practical?

– Is the main weakness a lack of a broad range of practical, manageable strategies for action?

• Are there rigorous monitoring and evaluation procedures in place?

• Does the process of monitoring, evaluation, prioritising and planning fit in with key development planning points in the school year?

Mid-course Task 32 (30 minutes)

This task deals with a critical analysis of a subject/department development/action/improvement plan using the criteria for good planning given above.

Working on your own or with a colleague(s):

• use the criteria for good action planning, above, to analyse one of the following plans, or your own

• ask the questions shown below and note your findings in the appropriate box

• share your findings with the rest of the group.

Questions	Comments
Are specific goals identified relating to pupil outcomes?	
Are they manageable (ie a small number of innovations)?	
Are they achievable (ie realistic, with appropriate steps)?	
Are resources identified?	
Are they time constrained?	
Are processes of monitoring and evaluation identified?	
Are there links to staff development and performance management?	
Other comments:	

Action Planning Exemplars

Case Study School – Secondary

The department analysed the most recent examination results in the autumn term. A series of lesson observations had been carried out by the HoD and other staff over the previous two terms. An evaluation of the outcomes of the self-evaluation activity set out the priorities to consolidate good practice and the focus for development that would form the basis of the subject development plan. The plan set out how these priorities would be achieved.

<table>
<tr><td align="center">Evaluation Outcomes</td></tr>
<tr><td>

Positives to consolidate (arising from best practice):

1. *Departmental team approach and commitment and willingness to pursue vision.*

2. *Excellence in teaching in some quarters – improvement in quality of teaching across the department and improvement in terms of more thoughtful planning, using schemes of work.*

3. *Teaching and learning with SEN/less practically able students.*

</td></tr>
<tr><td>

Focus for development (arising from less effective practice):

1. *Lesson planning – need for differentiated objectives for all key stages.*

2. *Clarity and effectiveness of sharing objectives with students and improved approach towards plenary.*

3. *Extending the more able.*

4. *Provision for those students who are performing practically beyond the NC – the Gifted and Talented.*

</td></tr>
</table>

Team Improvement Plan							
Department:	Physical Education – AST support						
Development priority/key issue:	Strategies for challenge and support						
What more should we aim to achieve?	**What must we do to make it work?**						
Objectives	Action/tasks	Persons responsible	Timeline (Dates)	Costs/ resources	Monitoring	Success criteria	Evaluation
Expand strategies for challenging and extension (KS 4 and 5)	Identification of individuals by CATs scores and abilities in theory groups	ANO(GCSE) ANP(A-level)	Nov 04	None	Evidence in registers Results from mock exams	Staff aware of student needs	Staff able to use this info effectively to inform planning
	Dept INSET	ANO	End of Nov 04	Monitoring and development time	Dept minutes	Understanding of relevance to improving attainment for all Feedback during INSET Informal discussions	Staff more confident with the material
	A-level obs by AST and by other A-level teachers Rotational basis with collaborative approach to planning for extension	ANO	Start Oct 04	Protected time	Feedback to HoD by AST	Informal/formal obs show use of strategies in lessons	Profile of results for GCSE and A-level show impact through higher numbers achieving A/*–B

Team Improvement Plan (continued)							
Expand strategies for challenging and extension (KS 4 and 5)	Create a bank of resources/tasks to challenge and extend	ANO	Feb 05	Photocopying	In place/ distributed	Informal/formal obs show use of strategies in lessons	Staff feed back as to effectiveness Resources continually updated

Development priority/Key issue:	Differentiated planning/clarity of objectives/plenaries

What more should we aim to achieve?	What must we do to make it work?

Objectives	Action/tasks	Persons responsible	Timeline (Dates)	Costs/ resources	Monitoring	Success criteria	Evaluation
Differentiated planning with clarity of objectives and plenaries	Dept INSET: focus on purpose of differentiation and how it is achieved	ANO (all dept)	End of Nov	AST time Monitoring and development time Dept minutes	Dept minutes	Understanding of relevance to improving attainment for all	Staff more confident and creative with material
	Lesson obs of Y 10 GCSE theory Rotate lead teacher and observe each session (Think method)	ANO ANP ANQ	Start Nov 04	Crashed ICT days	Feedback to HoD by AST	Degree of dialogue and sharing of good practice	Staff more confident with planning Lesson planning more effective for formal obs at GCSE

Team Improvement Plan (continued)							
Differentiated planning with clarity of objectives and plenaries (continued)	Collaborative planning for GCSE lessons – creation of key lesson plans	ANO	Dec 04	Monitoring and development time	Key lessons in place for each unit at GCSE	GCSE staff use lessons with success	Staff more confident with planning Lesson planning more effective for formal obs at GCSE
	Informal/formal obs of KS 4 practical lessons – paired	ANO ANP	Feb 05	AST time Obs time	Feedback to HoD by ANO and ANP	Lesson planning reveals differentiated outcomes	Improved GCSE practical scores

Development priority/Key issue:	Sharing of/planning differentiated objectives coupled with a more effective plenary, allowing better extension for the higher-attaining pupils' strategies for extension

What more should we aim to achieve?	What must we do to make it work?						
Objectives	**Action/tasks**	**Persons responsible**	**Timeline (Dates)**	**Costs/ resources**	**Monitoring**	**Success criteria**	**Evaluation**
Planning for student differences	Dept INSET – differentiated objectives	ANO	Oct 04	0	Dept minutes	Understanding of relevance to improving attainment for all	Very effective teaching for all formal observations at GCSE and A-level

Team Improvement Plan (continued)						
Differentitated planning/ clarity of objectives/ plenary

Strategies for challenging and extensions | Use crashed group time from IT days Y 10. AST leads session with other teacher observer Rotate next session | ANO | Start Oct 04 and then throughout the year | AST time/TA time/admin | Feedback to HoD by AST | Lesson planning at GCSE and A-level reveals different outcomes

Formal obs show use in lessons

AST aware of A-level and extension for higher-attaining pupils – HoD practice improves

Policy in place/evidence of improved provision (eg support network/ mentors/outside visitors) | Profile of results for GCSE – graph reflects targets more (more B–A*)

Less disparity between results for Unit 1 and Unit 3 at A-level

Feedback from ANP/other PE staff and Gifted and Talented students |
| | AST observes HoD deliver A-level – work together on planning for extension/plenary | AST/ANO | Start Sep 04 | AST time | Informal/ formal obs | | |
| | AST targets

A-level | AST | Jan 05 | AST time | Lessons planning of team | | |
| | ANP feedback to dept re G&T course specific to PE | ANP and SSCO (school sport coordinator) | Oct 04 | | ANP sees HoD | | |
| Improved provision for Gifted and Talented in KS 3 and KS 4 | Develop a policy and provision for those students whose practical abilities often go beyond NC | ANP and SSCO | Oct 04 | | Dept policy | | |

Review of the Secondary School Development Plan

Are specific goals identified relating to pupil outcomes?	*The success criteria include specific reference to improving GCSE and A-level results at A*–B, but there is no indication of how much improvement would constitute success.*
Are they manageable (ie a small number of innovations)?	*The goals set out are manageable and there are not too many in number.*
Are they achievable (ie realistic, with appropriate steps)?	*The goals set out are achievable and appropriate steps to take are set out clearly.*
Are resources identified?	*Resources are identified but not costed against a budget.*
Are they time constrained?	*Clear time constraints are included but most are in the short term.*
Are processes of monitoring and review identified?	*Processes of monitoring and review are included and are correctly distinct from one another. They include much direct observation and sharing of good practice.*
Are there links to staff development and performance management?	*There are clear links to staff development but less so to performance management.*

Other comments:

The development plan clearly arises from rigorous self-evaluation activity that includes analysis of pupils' results and performance and observation of lessons. The correct priorities appear to have been identified. There is some repetition in each development priority.

Primary School Development Plan	
Area for development:	*Physical Education:*
Area manager:	

2004 Achievements:

- *A successful Health and Fitness Week was carried out in school; children were made aware of the importance of health and fitness through a variety of lessons and games. The children participated in a healthy packed lunch competition and prizes were given to the best. The Newcastle Vipers visited the school to promote healthy lifestyles and fitness.*

- *The school achieved the Healthy School Award.*

- *Years 4, 5 and 6: Newcastle United's Football in the Community coaching.*

- *School football for boys in years 3, 4, 5 and 6 in the local league. Football was offered as an extra-curricular activity for girls in Years 5 and 6.*

- *School football teams entered the S...... Treat Final.*

- *School netball team entered the S...... Treat Final.*

- *School netball coaching for Years 4, 5 and 6.*

- *Cross-country lunchtime club offered to Year 5 children.*

- *Judo continued to be offered as an extra-curricular activity and this was extended to Years 3, 4, 5 and 6.*

- *A five-day intensive swimming course was offered to children in the October half-term.*

- *A 12-week dance programme from Dance Nation was offered to Key Stage 2 children, and will be concluded with a dance festival at Whitley Bay Playhouse this year. The children will perform their practised dance.*

- *Successful in school dance festival.*

- *A lunchtime club has been attended by Key Stage 2 children for 20 weeks. The children have been involved in team games, outdoor and indoor, in order to encourage good social skills and self-esteem.*

- *Acquisition of new PE equipment, for example, hoops, ropes, balls and mats.*

- *Continued in-service training for staff in gymnastics and games extended through the Primary Link Teacher (PLT) programme.*

- *Continuation of the PLT (sport coordinator programme).*

- *The use of a digital camera in lessons has provided children with a record of learning and a tool for evaluation.*

Financial Summary:

Items included cost of:

- *personnel time*
- *new stock/resources*
- *swimming*
- *equipment maintenance*
- *primary link teacher/staff development.*

Identified Needs	
2005/06	*To audit the range of extra-curricular activities for KS 1 pupils.*
2006/07	*To review pupil self-evaluation in PE – with potential use of CD-ROM Record of Achievement.*
2007/08	*To raise the fitness levels of all children in all year groups and to explore further use of the school grounds.*

Target 1 – In relation to the Ofsted report (Developing thinking skills) Title – Pupil Self-evaluation		
Task 1	*Ensure all lessons give the children the opportunity to self-evaluate and improve their skills, perhaps with the use of videoing for self-evaluation.*	Completion date: *Ongoing*
Task 2	*Give children the opportunity of working with children from different age groups through themed days and extra-curricular activities, in order to allow children to impact on each other's thinking. This will allow children to share ideas and develop their own thinking skills, which will have an impact on learning.*	Financial cost: *Materials*
Task 3	*Give the children the opportunity to plan and carry out their own warm-ups and cool-downs in order to develop their problem-solving and thinking skills. Encourage pupils to talk through processes they are using.*	Financial cost: *Personnel*

Target 2 – In relation to teaching and learning (use of assessment data/pupil tracking/fail-safe mechanisms) Title – Tracking in PE		
Task 1	Make and implement simple target and assessment sheets for each year group.	Completion date: *January 2006*
Task 2	Continue to use the PLT funding for staff participation in development courses.	Financial cost: *Materials*
Task 3	Children to set targets for themselves in PE in the form of a CD-ROM or written targets.	Financial cost: *Personnel*

Target 3 – In relation to Key Stage 1 and Key Stage 2 SATs (with focus on Gifted and Talented and value added) Title – Gifted and Talented in PE		
Task 1	Identify the G&T children in each year group and encourage them to join sport-centred extra-curricular activities.	Completion date: *Ongoing*
Task 2	Ensure that KS 1 children have more involvement in sporting extra-curricular activities, especially Year 2. Audit the extra-curricular activities to ensure that all children are given an equal opportunity to attend.	Financial cost: *Materials*
Task 3	Continuation of promoting positive pupil self-esteem in PE, which can have an impact on learning in other subjects.	Financial cost: *Personnel*

Target 4 – In relation to ICT (workforce reform/standards agenda) Title – ICT in PE		
Task 1	Identify the G&T children in each year group and encourage them to join sport-centred extra-curricular activities. Continuation of the use of a digital camera during lessons and extra-curricular activities.	Completion date: *Ongoing*
Task 2	Children to use the Internet to support their learning in PE – for example, creating health and fitness reports and posters.	Financial cost: *Materials*
Task 3	Children to use a video camera to record self-assessment and evaluation.	Financial cost: *Personnel*

Target 5 – In relation to opportunities for the whole child (oral language/high aspirations/parental involvement) Title – Developing the Whole Child		
Task 1	*Continue to develop sporting opportunities through extra-curricular activities in KS 1, through football run by Sure Start for reception and nursery children and a sport club to be set up for KS 1 children.*	Completion date:
Task 2	*During the science Health and Fitness Week, promote parents to being involved in encouraging their child to participate in sport outside of school.*	Financial cost: *Materials*
Task 3	*Year 6 children given opportunities to work with reception children to promote playing games at lunchtimes.*	Financial cost: *Personnel*

Success Criteria – In relation to Pupil Achievement

- *To have an increased range of extra-curricular activities available for KS 1 pupils.*
- *Most children who have previously not taken part in an extra-curricular sporting activity will have taken part in one this year. This will be achieved through an audit of children participating in sporting clubs.*
- *Assessment files will contain pupil targets and assessment data.*
- *CD-ROMs or a file of written targets will show pupils' own targets and achievements.*
- *Video and digital cameras will provide a portfolio of evidence of children's achievement and self-evaluation.*
- *Staff will have attended training courses.*
- *Time allocated to PE will be at least two hours in each key stage.*

Performance Indicators in Relation to the School Aims	
Aim 1	Lessons are carried out in a stimulating environment with good-quality PE resources.
Aim 2	PE lessons and 'good work' assemblies will provide individual recognition of personal achievements.
Aim 3	Self-evaluation will promote confident and independent learners through ICT.
Aim 4	Demonstration lessons carried out by experienced members of staff and planning will be monitored to ensure lessons are well planned and organised.
Aim 5	Team games and pupil evaluations of each other will promote respect for others and ensure that the school rules are adhered to.

Evaluation of Development:

Details provided related to the five targets.

Financial Summary:

Details provided.

Review of the Primary School Development Plan	
Are specific goals identified relating to pupil outcomes?	*There are clear indications of identified goals in each of the targets, with pupil outcomes in evidence and forming part of each target.*
Are they manageable (ie a small number of innovations)?	*The targets that are set fall within the parameters provided for guidance (eg three to five per year). There is a clear review of achievements for the previous year. As presented, the targets are manageable.*
Are they achievable (ie realistic, with appropriate steps)?	*Some of the tasks represent continuation work to develop particular aspects within the target. The steps utilised and previous reviews indicate that they are achievable.*
Are resources identified?	*Financial, physical and personnel resources are clearly identified for each target, with an overall financial summary (not included).*
Are they time constrained?	*Where this is appropriate, there are identified dates. Reference to previous plans clearly indicates that time constraints are applied as part of the process.*
Are processes of monitoring and review identified?	*There are clear success criteria in relation to pupil achievement and performance indicators which link to the school aims. There is an evaluation of work undertaken in the previous year's plan and this informs developments.*
Are there links to staff development and performance management?	*The evaluation of development clearly indicates some of the CPD opportunities provided.*

Other comments:

The plan follows a structure that is utilised for all subjects, ensuring that there is a consistency of approach across curriculum areas within the school. There is a clear linkage between the development plan and the aspirations the school has as a whole with regard to its target-setting process. Subject-specific performance indicators link to the school aims.

Financial details were provided in terms of the elements illustrated in the financial section – there was a substantial financial investment in physical education.

Evaluation of developments was undertaken in some detail (this was provided but included some personal details and was therefore removed from this document).

4.4 Drawing up an Improvement/Development/Action Plan Based on the Priorities Identified in Table 2, Unit I

Consider using your own or one of the following templates for action planning before starting the next task.

Exemplar Templates for Improvement/Development/Action Planning

Development Plan Framework					
Priority target:			Lead/monitoring personnel:		
Activity/Tasks	Personnel	Outcomes	Progress	Time	Resources

The following action plan format has been adapted from the National PESS Professional Development modules.

Action Planning

Specific Targets (Remember: these should be about the outcomes for learners)	Action (What are you to do to achieve your objective(s)?)	Signs of Success (What will you see learners doing when you have achieved your objective(s)?)	Collecting Information (How are you going to collect information to show whether you are achieving your signs of success?)
We want to:	We are going to:	When we have achieved our objective(s) we should see:	We are going to collect information by:

Post-course Task 33 (45 minutes)

In order to draw up an improvement/development/action plan, work from the **priorities for improvement identified in the SEF**, making sure that they are well focused on **raising standards, achievement, personal development and well-being**. The emphasis **must** be on **managing the improvement of learning and teaching**.

- Select an action-planning framework. Use your current framework or select a pro forma from the above examples.

- Set out manageable tasks and action to be taken within a set time frame and by whom.

- Identify what resources are required – costing them where possible.

- Identify the success criteria, which should be related to pupil outcomes. These should be specific and easily measurable.

- Identify what monitoring activity will take place, who will carry out the monitoring and when.

- Identify who will evaluate the findings of the monitoring.

45 mins	**Draw up an improvement/development plan based on two of the priorities you have identified. Work with a colleague/s.**

Assessment
For participants wishing to embark on accreditation, the completed development plan will need to be submitted to the course tutor within the time stipulated by the tutor.

4.5 Recap of the Self-evaluation and School Improvement Processes

Why Self-evaluate?

Effective self-evaluation is recognised as the key to school improvement and raising standards.

What is Self-evaluation?

It asks basic questions of the key outcomes and provision in a school:

- How well are we doing?

- How do we know?

- What do we need to do to improve?

It then uses this process to:

- monitor

- analyse

- evaluate

- plan

- act.

Refer back to Unit I for further information.

4.6 What Next? Personal Target Setting – Short, Medium and Long Term

It is essential that you apply what you have learnt from the course and have a clear idea of what you, personally, are going to do next.

Task 34 (15 minutes)

Working with a colleague(s), set out what you hope to have done and achieved in the short (one term), medium (one year) and long term (three years).

Short:

Medium:

Long:

Assessment

For participants wishing to embark on accreditation, the completed short-, medium- and long-term personal goals should be submitted to the tutor along with the improvement/development/action plan.

Appendix I: Primary School Case Study

Primary School Case Study Materials

The two DVDs included in the pack provide filmed lessons in both primary and secondary schools. The Year 7 lesson on the secondary school DVD may well be of interest to primary colleagues.

The material on the DVD includes:

1. a description of the school given by the head teacher

2. a description of a Year 2 class and lesson given by the AST/outreach coordinator

3. a Year 2 lesson on basic skills taught by the AST/outreach coordinator

4. evaluation and feedback on the lesson given by the class teacher to the AST/outreach coordinator

5. a description of a Year 6 class and lesson given by the class teacher

6. a Year 6 gymnastics lesson taught by the class teacher

7. evaluation and feedback on the lesson given by the AST/outreach coordinator to the class teacher.

Additional Material

The description of the school, the lessons and the feedback to teachers for each lesson are scripted below.

Lesson plans and evidence forms for each lesson are included. Each lesson has chapter points with a brief description of the content of each section.

1. A Description of the School Given by the Head Teacher

Summary

- An urban school on the edge of Sunderland.
- Approximately 500 children aged from 3 to 11.
- 7% of learners are entitled to free school meals but that does not reflect the intake.
- The intake comes from a much wider socio-economic group than the aforementioned 7% suggests.
- 10% of learners have special educational needs and there are four children with statements.
- Six children are from minority ethnic groups but all of them have English as a first language.
- The prior attainment of the learners is good.

Script

We generally do self-evaluation through auditing. Recently, the sports coordinator/PE coordinator did an audit for the staff and we found that there were certain areas where they were unhappy. They had some concerns and we started to supply specialists to augment the areas that they weren't very sure about.

We are very keen on PE in the school. We believe strongly, so strongly in fact that we tried for Active Mark Gold. We were successful. It reflected the practice that goes on in the school. We do 20 minutes of activity each morning, called Fitness for Learning – a scheme we brought from Noel Primary in Birmingham. We think it has calmed the children down. We think it has given the children a lot of purpose. It has become a big feature of the school. It also reflects the interest a lot of the staff have in PE and we offer 12 different sports during the life of a child in East Herrington Primary.

Our local comprehensive, Farringdon Community School, achieved Sports College Status. There were areas of our curriculum we weren't very sure about, so we consulted Farringdon and their outreach coordinator, Jill Sheridan, who has supplemented the areas where we think were weakened. We are not so good at gymnastics and we're not so good in dance in certain parts of the school – strong in other parts of the school – and Jill has been able to come on a weekly basis and help us enormously in the learning.

2. A Description of a Year 2 Class and Lesson Given by the AST/Outreach Coordinator

Script of the Filmed Discussion

I first started at Farringdon Community Sports College as outreach coordinator about two-and-a-half years ago, and the role there was to try and help teaching and learning in PE in the primary schools. The main focus for my work here is to do with progression – how to progress lessons as individual lessons from the beginning to the end and then also how to show how to progress through a series of lessons, from Lesson 1 to Lesson 8.

They're a lovely class – Year 2, which is aged 6–7. Today, we've got 27 pupils working out of a class of 30.

They're a mixed-ability group but we have assessed them using QCA criteria just on observation purely. We've put them into name bands:
- *Green – really achieving well above average.*
- *Blue – average ability.*
- *Red – working towards the criteria set.*

We roughly have seven or six who we think are achieving well and roughly five or six at the bottom who are working towards.

We have two children in the group with special educational needs and have a statement for that. It is really global learning difficulties and not specific to PE, although their gross motor skills are slightly behind the others.

We've been working on a programme of generic skills for about 14 weeks now. I think the progress they have made in the generic skills is quite outstanding.

The methodology is based on the generic skills of running, jumping and throwing, and from there, they're developed in different ways – for example, throwing under-arm, throwing over-arm to bouncing the ball – and we take that on a little bit every week, so that today we are doing dribbling skills, which they haven't done before. We use a system of going around stations and the idea is that they do these stations little and often as a drip, drip, drip method of learning the skill, so they don't just do it as a one-off one week and forget about it for the next six weeks.

Throughout the whole series of lessons, we've always been trying to help each other. Most of the skills that we've learnt could have been in pairs, where one does the skill and the other one watches, so that they learn exactly what is needed to improve that child.

It is an experimental system at the moment that we are trying out and it seems to work very efficiently. This system we're using is a pilot scheme from Edinburgh University.

The outcomes will be that all children are able to dribble the ball successfully and are able to take part in the game at the end of the session.

Today, I would like the observer to look at progression through the lesson. How I use the basketball skill through to the next station skill through the games part of the lesson, so that they can see a build-up of the use of the basketball skill.

Outline of the Class

- Year 2 class in June – aged 6 to 7 years.

- 27 pupils of mixed ability.

- Prior attainment (based on teachers' observations over a term and a half) – better than average.

- Two pupils with SENs.

- **Green name badges (higher-attaining pupils):**
  - Ashleigh (pale blue top and pink shorts)
  - Christopher (red England shirt and long red shorts)
  - Matthew K (red shirt)
  - Karina (white top and shorts)
  - Martha (white top and red-and-white striped shorts).

- **Blue name badges (average-attaining pupils):**
  - Luke, Eliot, Kye (white top), Matthew Je, Matthew Jo, Kane, James S, Tom (grey shirt – low academic ability), Ben (grey t-shirt and black shorts – high academic ability)
  - Hannah, Mollie, Amie, Bethany, Lauren, Megan, Jessica, Leilah, Sharman, Emma (low academic ability).

- **Red name badges (lower-attaining pupils and those with SENs):**
  - Dylan (white England shirt) – global learning difficulties (SEN)
  - James C (yellow shirt) – global learning difficulties and fine motor skills (SEN).

Prior Learning

- Generic games skills and movement skills – running, jumping, throwing.
- Twelfth lesson in a series of 14.

Focus for the Teacher Observer

- How well do pupils make progress in the lesson and over time?
- How well do pupils know and understand what they are trying to achieve?

Year 2 Lesson Plan – Basic Skills

Learning Objectives	Suggested Series of Activities
Pupils should learn: **Acquiring and Developing** To explore dribbling skills (basketball).	**Warm-up:** Pupils sitting around the whiteboard for objectives of the lesson. Corners warm-up using *Finding Nemo* characters. Pupils choose a card from the middle of the hall and then go to the appropriate corner to do the activity (eg Nemo corner will do galloping).
Selecting and Applying To select and apply these skills when moving around the hall, and in a game.	**Development:** Pupils to collect a ball and find a space. Pupils to make a big bubble by stretching. Pupils to perform some tricks with the ball (eg round the middle, through their legs). Are there any other tricks they can think of? Practise bouncing the ball. Use fingers; don't slap the ball. On command, stop and perform a 'trick'. Now moving in and out of each other around the hall. What do they need to use now (eg eyes)? On command, stop and perform a 'trick'.
Improving and Evaluating To observe each other and suggest ways of improving their skills.	**Composition:** In groups, pupils to move around the stations. Each station to be explained and groups move to that station. Stations to include a dribbling station, a running station, a jumping station and 'bouncing the ball on targets' and 'throwing at targets' stations, which will involve the pupils deciding themselves from where they will throw the shuttlecock. Teacher will be with the dribbling station. Game – 'Empty the Square'. Half the class in the square with a ball, dribbling it. One person without a ball, trying to knock all the other balls out of the square. What do people dribbling the ball have to do to stay in the game?
Fitness and Health To know that we need to warm up our bodies before we exercise.	**Cool-down/concluding activity:** Other half of group now play the game. Can you see anyone playing the game well? What are they doing? Recap on the objectives with the class. Have we achieved them?

3. Year 2 Lesson on Basic Skills Taught by the AST/Outreach Coordinator

Chapters and Lesson Activities

Year 2 – Basic Skills Lesson	
Time	**Chapters and Lesson Activities**
0 mins	Lesson objectives; warm-up activities
5 mins	Development of dribbling action – one ball per pupil
10 mins	Conclusion of dribbling work; setting up of activity stations
15 mins	Activities; observation and evaluation of throwing action
20 mins	Observation/evaluation of running and jumping; pupils self-challenging
25 mins	Working on stations; pupil feedback and evaluation
30 mins	Dribbling game; tactics introduced; half play, half observe
35 mins	Second group plays game; pupils watch/evaluate skills and tactics
45 mins	Review of lesson's objectives

Evidence Form

Inspector's OIN		Inspection number		Observation time				Observation type		L A D O
Year group(s)	Year 2	Grouping		**MC** SU SA SL O			BO GI **MI**	Present/NOR		
Subject codes		Support teachers/ assistants	SEN	T	S	EAL	T	S	Oth	T	S	Inspector's EF No	

(row: Subject codes / Support teachers/assistants with columns SEN T S | EAL T S | Oth T S | Inspector's EF No)

Name of teacher: *AST/outreach worker*	**Date:** *June*
Subject: *Games and movement skills*	**Year group and set:** *Year 2 mixed ability (MC)*
Observer: *Year 2 class teacher*	**Observation time:** *One hour*

Focus:	Learning objectives:
How well do pupils make progress within the lesson and over time? *How well do pupils know and understand what they are trying to achieve?*	*– to explore dribbling skills.* *– to apply these skills when moving around the hall and in a game.* *2 x SEN pupils – global LDs.* *5 x higher attaining pupils.* *Approximately 12th lesson in the series.*

Evaluation

What is helping pupils to learn, achieve and enjoy the lesson?	What is holding the pupils back from learning and achieving as well as they can?
Pupils are well motivated, perform confidently and enjoy the activities **because the teacher has established high expectations based on positive relationships and well-planned, challenging learning activities.** **They know what is expected of them at every point** because objectives for the lesson are shared at the start and referred to frequently. **All pupils have a chance to succeed and make progress** because the teacher sets clear, manageable goals and enables pupils to increase the challenge in their activities, as was seen when the pupils increased the distances from the targets in the throwing actions. Repetition from week to week is helping pupils to gain confidence and improve the control, accuracy and power of skills. Evaluation of others' performance is helping **pupils to improve their confidence** in recognising good performance and in communicating with others, but opportunities could be better structured. **Pupils make good progress in improving their technique** through the T's frequent, well-qualified feedback to individual pupils and the whole class (eg 'Well done!' followed by a description of what was well done). They benefit from the T's clear explanations based on secure knowledge and understanding, and her pertinent use of demonstration. Most of the lesson is well organised and moves on at a good pace so that pupils concentrate well and enjoy plenty of opportunity for physical activity.	Learning outcomes could be expressed a little more clearly and relate to outcomes. **Do pupils know what 'explore' and 'apply' mean?** For example, 'By the end of the lesson: • you will be able to dribble a ball at walking/running speed with control Though pupils understand that they will evaluate each other's work, this is not identified as a learning outcome. Nor are objectives relating to knowledge and understanding of HRE. **LOs are not differentiated and so it is not clear what the highest-attaining pupils might achieve in the lesson.** Pupils could be given more responsibility for setting up the equipment and putting it away. Though questioning is used well overall, some questioning is closed and could demand more of pupils, especially HA pupils. Few questions are targeted towards individual pupils. More encouragement could be given to pupils to increase the challenge within each activity (eg where some pupils began to develop different jumps, jumps with a turn or a shape). Where the T supported peer evaluation, pupils were often successful but some found it difficult to concentrate on performance and evaluation, so evaluation activities need clearer structuring, particularly for LA/SEN pupils. Missed opportunity to use the whiteboard to set out key technical language. The organisation of some activities (dribbling and running) leads to some queuing and pace of activity slows.

Are there any differences between groups of pupils?

Boys and girls make equally good progress in improving their skills but more girls are more confident in giving feedback to each other. Both pupils with SENs and LA pupils make good progress in improving their skills and gaining personal confidence. HA pupils are making sound progress in improving their skills and techniques.

Evidence Form (continued)

Summary of the main points:

This is a good lesson, where all pupils enjoy making good progress in improving skills of balance and poise, personal confidence and communication skills. Pupils learn at a good rate because good teaching sets high expectations of pupils' learning, behaviour and conduct. Well-planned, progressively challenging learning activities help pupils to gain confidence. **Frequent feedback to pupils helps them to know what they must do to improve.** *Peer evaluation helps pupils to improve their communication skills.* **Progress over time is good** *because pupils build confidence in their skills. Learning outcomes could be expressed more clearly and* **differentiated.** *Some evaluation activities could be better structured.*

Judgement on the overall quality of the lesson:	I – Outstanding 4 – Inadequate	2

Use for grades if there is sufficient evidence:

Standards	Progress	Personal development	Teaching	Curriculum	Care, guidance and support	Leadership and management
	2	2	2	2		

Particular evaluations relating to safety, health, enjoyment, contribution to the community and economic well-being:

Pupils are learning how to prepare for exercise safely and work alongside others safely. Pupils are learning how to maintain health through exercise, though this is not emphasised specifically in this lesson. Well-planned activities help pupils to enjoy the activity. Opportunity for frequent practice and consequent improvement leads to building of self-confidence and enjoyment. Good emphasis on working together helps pupils to develop essential basic social skills.

Health and safety:

Risk assessment of the lesson and of the filming had been carried out.

The following outstanding health and safety issues were identified by **baalpe***: long hair of pupil not safely tied back; some stretching (ie touching toes) contraindicated (potentially damaging to lower back); most pupils in bare feet but at least one pupil in footwear – 'mixed economy' not advisable when pupils are working in a restricted space; what appears to be an unsecured ladder leant against wall in far corner of hall; throwing activity – better that pupils all throw together and then collect together, rather than individually.*

Evaluation of the Lesson Evidence Form

- Appropriate balance between evaluation and description, with one or two useful specific examples that will help when it comes to feedback.

- Good link between the features of teaching and their effect on learners' progress and learning.

- It could have been more clearly focused on the two focus areas.

- There is a flavour of the subject – you know it is a PE lesson.

- There is plenty of useful information in the context box.

- Judgements appear to be correct, looking at the balance of strengths and weaknesses.

- There were some useful suggestions for improvement in the second column, which should help the feedback to be constructive and helpful.

- The layout may be helpful in setting out what takes learning forward or holds it back, but it leads to some repetition and possible confusion. It may be better to write positives and negatives alongside each other (ie 'This…is good. However, this…holds back learning.').

- It is rather lengthy and perhaps not focused enough.

4. Evaluation and Feedback on the Lesson Given by the Class Teacher (T) to the AST/Outreach Coordinator (Observer: O)

Script

O: *Thank you for letting me watch the lesson...I thought the lesson went well. How did you feel it went?*

O: *There were lots and lots of strengths...good progression. Pupils used their initiative.*
Good discussion between teacher and observer. Good reference to individual pupils by observer and teacher.

O: *Can we cater more for the more able and SEN pupils and have even more effect?*

O: *One thing I possibly thought for the more able...*
Observer offers an idea as to how to further challenge the more able pupils.

O: *There was also progression from our previous lessons...*
Positive comment about progression over time.
Discussion between teacher and observer about progression and reasons for it.

O: *I thought also, within the lesson, that you could see progression...introduced tactics...*

T: *This reflects on how I could have improved the use of the whiteboard to emphasise literacy.*

O: *We've talked about good progression but it has to be said...*
Observer feeds back features of good teaching:
  • Good breakdown of skills into easy-to-follow stages.
  • Frequent demonstrations and good praise, highlighting what is good.

T: *I do like to use the children as examples...*
Discussion between observer and teacher on good practice in using children as examples.

O: *Also in good teaching...*
Feedback on the good continuous assessment and encouragement of self-assessment and peer assessment...

Observer asks the teacher how she feels the peer assessment went.
Good self-evaluation of teaching by the teacher herself on this issue. Recognises the need to develop pupils' ability to evaluate each other.

O: *Another very good teaching point was the pace and the fun of the lesson.*
Feedback to teacher on good pace of lesson.

O: *The one thing that could possibly help to keep the pace going...*
Observer feeds back suggestion to increase pace even more.

O: *Summary of strengths and areas for improvement include:*

- *good learning*

- *new skills taught and developed*

- *evaluated performance*

- *analysis*

- *good teaching:*
  - *– Skills were taught well and the lesson was well structured.*
  - *– The children were challenged and they had achieved something by the end of the lesson.*
  - *– Clear objectives were referred to at the end of the lesson.*
  - *– Ways forward, catering more for more able and less able, were suggested.*
  - *– Vocabulary was included.*

Evaluation of the Feedback

- Very clear and succinct.

- Well focused on pupils' outcomes of achievement and enjoyment.

- Put the teacher at ease.

- Stressed the positives first and sensitively introduced areas for development.

- Gave plenty of opportunity for professional dialogue.

- Gave clear judgements but not always clear how the Ofsted criteria were used.

---

5. A Description of a Year 6 Class and Lesson Given by the Class Teacher

Script

They're a Year 6 class aged 10 to 11. Normally, there are 27 in the class. There'll be 22 children performing today, with one child who is not participating but is actually helping in the class. There are normally 16 boys and 11 girls. Today, we've got 14 boys and 10 girls. [Actual numbers are 12 boys and 10 girls.]

We've got three children who are actually Gifted and Talented sportsmen, mainly in team games and football. One child is Gifted and Talented for gymnastics. We have two SEN children, both with statements. One child has multiple myopathy, which affects his fine and gross motor skills, and he tires very easily. The other child has language and communication difficulties, so needs things explaining to her perhaps more than once.

The ability groups that they will be arranged into: the less able children will be working on red mats, average ability children will be working on light blue mats and the more able children will be working on navy mats.

In my opinion, the class are working at an above-average level on the whole in gymnastics.

Looking back over what they have done in gymnastics in the past, by Year 5, they had actually achieved balancing on different parts of the body, so we have moved on this year to partner balancing.

The objectives for this lesson are to explore counterbalances and then to be able to put together a sequence of counterbalances with a partner, working on either two, three, four or five movements. The more able, I am hoping, will be able to put them together in a sequence using a series of moves to actually join their balances together. The less able will come up with three counterbalances.

The children are actually going to assess them themselves. What they are actually going to be doing is look at another group's sequence and be able to suggest improvements on how they can improve their sequence.

Q: *You've had some outside input, haven't you, into PE in the school? Could you tell me a little bit about that?*

An outreach coordinator from our feeder secondary school at Farringdon who is available to come and work with teachers on how they can improve their own teaching skills as far as PE is concerned.

It has worked very well because, as a primary school teacher, you tend to really have a specialism yourself but because you are teaching the whole of the primary curriculum, it is really useful to have another specialist come in and be able to work with you to improve your own teaching in an area that you feel needs developing.

Q: *Can you tell me what sort of focus you expect the observer to hone in on today?*

I'm hoping that Jill's going to be looking at how well the children are able to assess their own performances and the performances of others and how they can actually improve them.

Outline of the Class

- Year 6 class in June – aged 10 to 11 years.
- 22 pupils of mixed ability; one non-participant.

HAPs – Dark blue mats	AAPs – Light blue mats	LAPs – Red mats
Daniel and Connor (both identified as G&T in sport) Miriam and Emily Georgina and Jasmine Robyn and Alexandra	Matti and Jake Paul and Satveer Stephen, Jamie and Jonathon Louise and Vicki	Sanvir and Owen Victoria (SEN) and Robert (SEN)

- Prior attainment (based on teachers' observations) – better than average.
- Two pupils with SENs.

Prior Learning

- Previous work in Year 5 on balance.
- Second lesson of eight-week unit on balancing.

Focus for the Teacher Observer

- How well the pupils can assess their own and others' performance.
- How well they make improvements.

Year 6 Lesson Plan – Gymnastics

Learning Objectives	Suggested Series of Activities
Pupils should learn the following: **Acquiring and Developing** To explore counterbalance.	**Warm-up:** Explain objectives for the lesson at the whiteboard. Moving around the hall. On command, stop and perform front or back support. Working with a partner, select appropriate stretches for arms, legs and trunk.
Selecting and Applying To choose three, four or five counterbalances and link them together in a sequence.	**Development:** Using whiteboard, explain **counterbalance** (ie when both pupils are held or supported in a position that would be impossible to hold if your partner moved away). Ask pupils to experiment on mats some of the counterbalance pictures on the wall. Each balance to be performed slowly and carefully. Good body tension must be shown throughout.
Improving and Evaluating To observe others and help them to improve their performance.	**Composition:** Children to choreograph a sequence of moves to include three, four or five counterbalances. Teacher to give ideas of areas they could improve, and to put these ideas on the whiteboard (eg good body tension, balance held for three seconds, effective linking movements). Once sequence has been performed, the two observers will give feedback to the two performers. They will then change over. What actions would be good linking movements (eg roll, cartwheel, jump, turn, twist)? In a group of four, two pupils perform while two observe and help improve.
Fitness and Health To understand that a warm-up is important in gymnastics. To be able to select appropriate stretches in their own warm-up.	**Cool-down/concluding activity:** Teacher to ask for some suggestions of improvement that observers made. All pairs to finish by performing the sequence again with the improvements in.

6. A Year 6 Gymnastics Lesson Taught by the Class Teacher

Chapters and Lesson Activities

Time	Chapters and Lesson Activities
0 mins	Lesson objectives; warm-up activity builds on earlier work
5 mins	Stretching activities, partly student led; pupils get out mats
10 mins	Counterbalance introduced/tried out; teacher feeds back
15 mins	Pupils evaluate a counterbalance
20 mins	Counterbalance sequence task, differentiated for higher attainers
25 mins	Sequence building continues; teacher works with mid-attainers
30 mins	Teacher works with mid-attainers; sequence work continues
35 mins	Pupils observe and evaluate sequences – teacher assists
40 mins	Teacher/class discuss evaluation; sequence building continues
45 mins	Review of lesson's objectives

Evidence Form

Inspector's OIN		Inspection number		Observation time		60		Observation type		L A D O
Year group(s)	6	Grouping		**MC** SU SA SL O			BO GI **MI**	Present/NOR		
Subject codes	PE		Support teachers/ assistants	SEN	T	S	EAL	T	S	Oth	T	S	Inspector's EF No		

(continued)

Subject codes	PE	Support teachers/ assistants	SEN	T	S	EAL	T	S	Oth	T	S	Inspector's EF No

Focus:

How well do pupils assess each other's performance and help each other to improve?

How well does the teaching ensure progress within the lesson and over time?

Context:

LOs –To explore counterbalance; to choose three, four or five counterbalances and link together in a sequence; to observe others and help to improve their performance.

2 x SEN pupils – global LDs.

Second lesson in the series of eight.

Evaluation:

• Pupils know what is expected of them, lesson objectives are made clear and the T refers to them frequently.

• All the pupils show positive attitudes and behave very well because the T has well-established, positive relationships with them, based on high expectations of conduct and learning.

• Pupils show a good level of independence in their learning. They readily make use of the well-prepared resources, such as the posters, and they are confident in their abilities to support and help each other. (Focus)

• Pupils know how to warm up and some HA pupils are confident in leading.

• Missed opportunity to challenge pupils to learn names of muscles and to link warm-up activity to gymnastics.

• Some pupils not corrected when carrying out stretches incorrectly, reflecting limited K&U of the T.

• Well-planned series of activities, including the use of pupil demonstration, build up pupils' confidence. Pupils encouraged to think for themselves what the good features of CBs are, though effective questioning could be more 'open'. It does build on their responses, improving their understanding.

– Limitations of T K&U evident in explanation of balance and CB. Some confusion between paired support balances and CB. (Could explore basic principles of balance more, for example base, C of G, stillness and differences within CBs, eg pushing and pulling).

• Pupils use the language of the subject confidently because the T explains it well.

• Good differentiation of activities so that HA pupils are challenged to produce more difficult CBs, though they do not develop linking actions as well as they might.

• Pupils are successful in helping each other to improve because they understand what is needed to improve and they have plenty of opportunity to observe each other. HA pupils are confident and able to draw on the full range of criteria.

– LA and MA pupils do not always recall the criteria and would benefit from more structured evaluation tasks.

• Pupils with SENs make good progress. They understand the tasks. They benefit from working alongside HA pupils.

• Pupils maintain good levels of concentration. They work hard and enjoy the challenge.

– However, towards the end of the sequencing, some pupils begin to lose concentration and the T does not pick this up because of her close involvement with groups. This also prevents her from keeping an overview of the whole class – an H&S concern.

– Plenary was rushed and could have involved more of the pupils. However, overall, the T uses her K&U of the pupils' prior learning and capabilities well, to ensure that they are challenged or supported (eg different questions were posed to individuals, matching their capabilities).

– Missed opportunities to develop linking actions within the sequences meant that some sequences were limited in length and overall interest.

Summary of main points:

• A high proportion of the class work at a better level than expected for their age. They plan and combine series of actions thoughtfully, showing good control, though the range of linking actions is limited. They analyse performance well, reflecting a good level of understanding, using technical terms confidently.

• All pupils are suitably challenged and make good progress, though some limitations in T K&U limit the depth of understanding.

• Good teaching resulted in good rates of learning for all pupils. Good assessment for learning evident in T's knowledge of the pupils, well-matched activities and questions, clear objectives that the pupils understood and good involvement of pupils in recognising how much progress they had made towards them.

• Very good behaviour, positive attitudes, pupils working well in pairs.

Evidence Form (continued)						

Areas for improvement:

Develop subject K&U of teacher; ensure position in class enables a view of all pupils; restructure feedback to tasks to support LA and MA pupils; focus on improving 'linking' actions to improve fluency of the sequences.

Judgement on the overall quality of the lesson (Leave blank when not a lesson) I = Outstanding, 4 = Inadequate	2

Use for grades if there is sufficient evidence:

Standards	Progress	Personal Development	Teaching	Curriculum	Care, Guidance and Support	Leadership and Management
	2	I	2			

Particular evaluations related to safety, health, enjoyment, contribution to the community and economic well-being:

• *Overall, pupils are working in a safe environment.*

• *T's hair should be tied back and no jewellery should be worn.*

• *Limited T K&U of counterbalance and tension.*

• *Good levels of pupil activity and enjoyment.*

• *Very good opportunities to work cooperatively and independently.*

Evaluation of the Lesson Evidence Form

• Good balance of evaluation and description – we know this is a gymnastics lesson.

• Impact of teaching on pupils' learning and progress is made clear.

• Reference to focus is there – though perhaps not enough is made of the progress of HA pupils in the summary and in contributing to the overall judgement. Had HA pupils made good progress?

• Context box could give more information about the prior attainment of the class and previous learning.

• Layout of lesson EF allows strengths and weaker areas to be reported alongside each other. Use of the '–' signs helps to indicate the weaker areas. Summary of areas for improvement will help with feedback.

• Overall judgement may well be correct – but is questionable in light of the comments re the progress of HA pupils, the lack of progress in developing linking actions for all pupils and the H&S concerns.

• Not all boxes at the top of the EF are completed – may lead to missed points such as attendance, nature of group, presence of a TA.

• Rather lengthy with perhaps too much detail.

7. Evaluation and Feedback on the Lesson from the AST/Outreach Coordinator to the Class Teacher

Script

O = Observer
T = Teacher

The observer begins by thanking the teacher and providing an overall summary and question to the teacher on how she thought it went. The teacher responds.

O: *I think we'll go on to the strengths…differentiation*
The observer asks for clarification and the teacher makes good contribution.

O: *Any other areas that you feel you could challenge the HAs…warm-up?*
T: *Naming muscle groups – HA pupils*

O: *Pupils knew what was expected of them…good use of resources…problem solving.*
The teacher responds.

O: *Questions whether all pupils understood what counterbalance was.*
Discussion with T. Recognition of need to develop pupils' understanding of balance and counterbalance.

O: *Pupils were given plenty of opportunity for understanding and thinking. There was good use of the whiteboard.*

O: *How did you feel the peer assessment went?*
Good discussion between the teacher and observer.
Assessment – peer assessment discussion.
AFI – structure feedback for pupils. Look for one thing, two things to change…

O: *Use of someone not taking part in the lesson. Good discussion.*
The observer discusses plenary; the teacher agrees it was rushed.
The observer summarises the peer assessment and lesson.

Evaluation of the Feedback

- Clear and succinct.
- Reasonable focus on the progress and achievement of the pupils but sometimes issues raised about teaching without making clear what the impact is on learning and achievement.
- Gives useful feedback on the focus for the evaluation.
- Puts the teacher at ease but also not afraid to raise areas for development.
- Gives the teacher plenty of opportunity for professional discussion.

Appendix II: Secondary School Case Study

Secondary School Case Study Materials

The secondary case study material is set in a comprehensive school in Nottinghamshire. The material on the DVD includes a Year 7 and a Year 10 lesson. The Year 6 lesson will also be of interest to secondary colleagues:

1. A description of the school given by the head teacher.

2. A description of a Year 7 class and lesson given by the head of PE.

3. A Year 7 athletics lesson taught by the head of PE.

4. Evaluation and feedback on the lesson from the AST to the class teacher.

5. A description of a Year 10 class and lesson given by the AST.

6. A Year 10 GCSE theory lesson taught by the AST.

7. Evaluation and feedback of the Year 10 GCSE theory lesson from the head of PE to the AST.

Additional Material

The description of the school, the lessons and the feedback to teachers of each lesson are scripted below.

Lesson plans and evidence forms for each lesson are included. Each lesson has chapter points with a brief description of the content of each section.

1. A Description of the School Given by the Head Teacher

Script

We're a mixed comprehensive school with 1500 pupils – boys and girls, of course. We are in a small market town of Southwell, in a largely rural part of Nottinghamshire.

The ability profile of the youngsters is skewed from the middle to the upper end. It is a fairly affluent area. That means that what we need to do is make sure that we teach good lessons and have high aspirations for our pupils. Otherwise, average teaching can produce good results but not good enough results.

PE was a subject which, in 1995, when we had our first Ofsted inspection, was declared to have an unsatisfactory department. I guess the department had always run a good range of extra-curricular activities but there hadn't been a sufficiently robust approach to teaching and learning. So that was a subject, it was the only subject, that was unsatisfactory and we've needed to make sure that there has been a good, robust journey of improvement – departmental improvement for PE.

We've got a good team under our current Head of Department, Jules Foster. There has been a really good period of development and now it is an outstanding department, so we are really proud of what our PE staff have achieved, but it has been achieved by a really good focus, as I say, on high-quality teaching and learning.

PE, as I said, was unsatisfactory in 1995. In 2000, although we were achieving well as a school, the whole school was judged to be underachieving. We were given that unwelcome category. It was really useful to us because what it made us do was really focus upon school self-evaluation and continuous improvement across the school, and in many ways, the success that PE had enjoyed earlier, to move things on in terms of standards and quality of provision, gave us the model from which to develop our whole-school approaches. And, in fact, now those approaches to school self-evaluation have left us in a very good position for the new inspection framework.

To describe them simply, they are based on regular classroom observation but no-one is observed more than three times in a year, so that we need to make sure that our observations count. Alongside observation and feedback, there is a formal termly evaluation by the subject leader into standards and quality of provision in the department, and that looks at data. It looks at individual pupil performance. In those subjects where it is appropriate, there will be work sampling. There will be interviews with students to get their views as learners. There is a regular slot every Wednesday at 2.30, when our pupils go home early, where all our staff get together in departmental teams to discuss teaching and learning. At the end of each term, there is a formal evaluation – what is working well and what needs further attention. What needs further attention becomes a team improvement plan for the next term. That then becomes the subject for classroom observation and also that weekly staff-development slot. Then it's for the subject leader to manage that process, and then there is a member of the senior team, who is a line manager, if you like, linked to the department, who holds the subject leader accountable for what they are doing in terms of self-evaluation. That process is now embedded.

2. A Description of a Year 7 Class and Lesson Given by the Head of PE

Outline of the Class

- 28 pupils – 11- and 12-year-olds.
- 15 boys and 13 girls, taught as a mixed-ability group.
- SEN – eight identified as on the SEN school database: four have IEPs and four are in the school's category of 'Be Aware'.
- Two G&T: Joe and Tom. CAT scores 120+.
- One from EMG.
- Ability overall is above average in PE.
- Pupils' listening skills were initially poor and this impacted on behaviour and attainment. Have improved and now they are good.

The pupils followed a nine-week athletics activity module two terms before this lesson (September), and a nine-week fitness module in April. During the AA module, pupils explored jumping for distance and how to combine jumps in different ways. At the moment, this group are following a module of swimming and a module of striking games.

Script

It's a Year 7 class. They arrived in September at Minster, so they're between 11 and 12 years of age. It's a mixed-ability group and there are 28 students in the class: 15 boys and 13 girls.

They have done a variety of activities up until this date but, in Year 7, it tends to be a lot more generic and a holistic approach about the fundamental skills that students require. I'm teaching triple jump or that kind of activity today but, earlier on in Year 7, they will have done jumping for distance and exploring combining jumps and those kind of things.

When they first arrive, all that prior attainment is judged from my conversations with them about the sports that they're interested in and the things that they have done – because they come from a range of at least 40 feeder schools – and then my teacher assessments in the lesson. Then, after every module, I record on an individual record card each student across the four areas of the National Curriculum. I write down what their strengths are and what areas they could improve upon, and that builds up a kind of picture of a student over time.

There'll be a lot of variety in what I do, so that I try to meet the different learning styles of those students. And, also, I'll try to use different times on activities. Some will be short and some will be longer, with periods to consolidate, which some students prefer. There'll be demonstrations that some students prefer, but I'll try to really emphasise a really active approach because I want to keep the physical inside of physical education, but I'll try to have so much variety, not only in my questioning, but the activity and the thinking skills that they do and the strategy I'll use in my delivery style, in the expectation from them, whether they work independently or whether they work in pairs or in groups. So that hopefully, within that lesson, there are not just one but many opportunities where a child feels that they're grasping on to the way they like to learn and that they're having some success and progress.

Two, really, have been identified by the school as being Gifted and Talented because their CATs scores are in the 30s and one is nearly on 40 and can be considered really Gifted and Talented. In terms of physical education, we identify those we feel are Gifted and Talented, not just within our curriculum, but perhaps Gifted and Talented in rock climbing or rowing or basketball – perhaps something that they don't do earlier on in school. We only really formalise that at the end of Year 8 but I think that I have got four within my group that are showing potential to be on that list now. In terms of ethnic minorities, I have one student who would be considered to be from an ethnic minority background.

I really want them to understand the factors that really affect their performance in triple jumping so that they can actually improve their performance. So, at the end of the lesson, I'll want them to be able to identify those factors to me. Now, some of them will be able to articulate that really well because of their academic ability, but I'm hoping that some can not only articulate it but really show that in their performance too.

Q: *Can you tell me what the observer should be focusing on?*
> *Well, we've been working all this year at looking at thinking skills, so it's thinking skills without a dependence on paper resources.*

> *But, also, schools are trying to use the CATs scores of students in a more meaningful way. I'm trying to make notes in my own choice of activity and things I want them to learn, to have reference to how they best learn according to their profile or the aspects of their particular profile that they need to develop to make them learn better.*

Pupils		
Above Average Academic Ability	**Average Academic Ability**	**Below Average Academic Ability**
2　Vincent	1　Benson	7　Thomas
3　Sam Be	6　Emma	12　Amy
4　Lauren	9　Louise	19　Joanne
5　Sam Bu	11　Holly	27　Jack
8　Joe (very high academic ability)	16　Kayleigh	
	17　Ollie	
13　Jonathan	23　Jack	
14　Beth	24　Chloe	
15　Tom (very high academic ability)	25　Adam	
	28　Sam	
18　Grace		
20　Edward		
21　Jessica		
22　Beth		
26　Christopher		

Year 7 Lesson Plan – Athletics

Year group: *7/8*	Week no: *1*	Unit: *Athletic Activity*

Learning objectives – what you hope the students will learn:
- *To be able to combine jumps with increasing fluency.*
- *To be able to identify factors that make performance effective.*
- *To perform a recognisable TJ using the TJ grid.*
- *To evaluate performance and recognise strengths and weaknesses in performance.*

Starter/introduction:

S. Activities to combine actions (at least two, no more than four – remember so can repeat).

Prior learning – last time, combination jumps. What would you see if the combination was fluent?

Develop idea of importance of balance and how achieved.

So what? Fluency/balance?

Choose – combine two hop/bound (same), one to the other. Are you fluent and on balance?

Development (most):

Predict outcome of T throwing a ball.

Write or discuss. Convert to a diagram or graph. Test then review.

Q. What happened to height? Speed? Why the changes?

Impact on distance between bounces got shorter.

Does fluency affect distance? Why? (Maintains/helps speed.) Arms?

Trajectory of ball. Tennis ball v juggling ball. (Ducks and Drakes, Hurdles link.)

Standing TJ. If balanced/fluent/flat ➤ 3–5-step approach.

Establish criteria for assessment – fluent, balanced, phasing, maintain speed (flat), order.

Conclusion (plenary):

Discuss > rewrite/draw graph. Convert for TJ instead of ball.

F + F + F = Fluency

Differentiation (all):

Hop straight leg–impact safety

Two combinations

Extension (some):

Breaking effect of foot too far ahead – breaks speed.

Greater number of combinations of hop/bounce ➤ test. Fluency/balance maintained?

Grouping strategies:

Individual, pair and share, groups of six.

Learning outcomes – assessing extent to which students have met learning objectives:

- *Identify balance, fluency and maintaining speed throughout as factors for effective performance re distance. To understand cause and effect.*

- *To show these elements according to ability in performance.*

Non-participants' role:	**Language for learning:**
• *All perform.*	*Fluency* *trajectory*
• *Evaluation/judging/feedback.*	*Rhythm* *momentum*
• *Improved observation skills.*	*Balance*

Resources:	**Health and fitness:**
• *Whiteboards and pens.*	*Not a direct focus.*
• *Tennis ball and juggling ball.*	**Safety:**
• *Marker cones.*	*Avoid too many repetitions.*
• *LJ equipment.*	*Flat foot landing – not toe!*
• *Skipping ropes.*	*Limit run-up to a few steps (skidding).*

Outline of Year 7 Athletics Lesson

Time	Chapters and Lesson Activities
0 mins	Warm-up; recap of previous learning; today's objectives
5 mins	Discussion and observation of fluent movement – skipping
10 mins	Jumping practice to improve fluency and balance; feedback
15 mins	Further jumping practice (limited to three); distance estimated
20 mins	Teacher-led review of jumps/factors affecting performance
25 mins	Pupils work on improving momentum and distance
30 mins	Maintaining speed and momentum; demonstration with ball
35 mins	Pupils practise jumps in pit; teacher reviews pupils' work
45 mins	Cool-down stretches; observer interaction with pupil

Lesson Evidence Form

<table>
<tr><td colspan="11" align="center">Evidence Form</td></tr>
<tr>
<td>Inspector's OIN</td><td></td>
<td>Inspection number</td><td></td>
<td colspan="2">Observation time</td>
<td colspan="2">60</td>
<td>Observation type</td>
<td colspan="2">L A D O</td>
</tr>
<tr>
<td>Year group(s)</td><td>7</td>
<td>Grouping</td>
<td colspan="4">MC SU SA SL O</td>
<td colspan="2">BO GI MI</td>
<td>Present/NOR</td><td></td>
</tr>
<tr>
<td>Subject codes</td><td>PE</td>
<td>Support teachers/ assistants</td>
<td>SEN</td>
<td>T</td><td>S</td>
<td>EAL</td>
<td>T</td><td>S</td>
<td>Oth</td>
<td>T</td><td>S</td>
<td>Inspector's EF No</td><td></td>
</tr>
</table>

Focus (ie main purpose of the inspection activity):

How well does the teaching improve pupils' thinking skills?

How well does the teaching take account of pupils' different cognitive abilities?

Context: *Athletics – Triple Jump*

LOs: *To be able to combine jumps with increasing fluency; to be able to identify factors (balance, fluency and speed) that make performance effective; to show these elements according to ability in performance; to understand cause and effect; to evaluate performance and recognise strengths and weaknesses.*

Prior attainment: *Overall **above average** in PE. G&T – 2 boys based on CATs scores. Four with potential to be on G&T list for PE.*

SEN – 4 with IEPs – MLD, 4 on school's 'Be Aware' system – MLD.

First lesson in triple jump since nine-week generic athletics/fitness module taught in Sept.

Evaluation:

- Pupils enjoy the lesson and make good progress in understanding some of the factors affecting performance because the teaching is well planned and takes pupils through well thought-out series of learning steps.

- Relationships are good and pupils work hard and are 'on task' throughout the lesson. They work very well in pairs and groups supporting one another and giving advice sensitively. They respond well to the T's high expectations of conduct, depth of thinking and improvement.

- Pupils are clear about what is expected of them because the T makes LOs very clear and refers to them frequently, helping pupils to understand how well they are doing.

- Pupils know how well they are doing in relation to the LOs and they know what they must do to improve because the T gives frequent helpful feedback to individuals and the whole class.

- An imaginative range of different learning activities caters for pupils' differing learning styles.

- The T effectively encourages pupils to think about what they are doing, despite some closed questioning. Pupils are often challenged (eg to work out the features of good performance for themselves).

- Pupils' thinking is well developed through the T's skilful questioning and range of problem-solving/probing questions.

- Pupils of differing prior attainment make good progress because of the T's targeted questioning and the mixed composition of the group work.
- Lengthy discussions sometimes slow the level of physical activity.
- Not clear how much pupils learnt through demo of bouncing ball. Some confusion as to how to record their discussions slowed pace.
- Some important teaching points not developed (eg flat feet to help maintain balance).
- Not enough attention paid to regular raking of pit, so that some pupils landing on hard areas of sand.

- Most pupils understand some of the factors affecting triple jump and around four or five have secure technique using short run-up. The rest of the class made good progress in understanding what is needed and are linking jumps fluently but not always in the correct order. Pupils recognise the factors affecting performance.

Evidence Form (continued)

Summary of main points:

• *Overall, progress is good.*

• *Well-planned teaching uses a good variety of learning activities that take pupils' different ways of learning into account.*

• *Pupils are effectively challenged to think for themselves and share their ideas with each other.*

• *HA pupils and those with SENs make good progress.*

• *The level of physical activity slows during some lengthy discussion times.*

• *Some H&S issues need correcting.*

• *Overall a good lesson because the pupils made good progress. They enjoyed the lesson, behaving very well and cooperating very well with each other.*

Judgement on the overall quality of the lesson (Leave blank when not a lesson) I = Outstanding, 4 = Inadequate	2

Use for grades if there is sufficient evidence:

Standards	Progress	Personal Development	Teaching	Curriculum	Care, Guidance and Support	Leadership and Management
	2	I	2			

Particular evaluations related to safety, health, enjoyment, contribution to the community and economic well-being:

• *H&S issues: Benefits of warm-up lost when followed by a lengthy discussion; full approach to triple jump on grass not recommended; pit not dug and raked sufficiently so some pupils – especially LAs – landing on hard sand; subject K&U of T overlooks important teaching point that would aid achievement of balance and stability.*

• *Pupils actively enjoying lesson. Clear regular enjoyment of PE lessons.*

• *Good opportunities for pupils to work cooperatively and to improve communication skills.*

Evaluation of the Lesson Evidence Form

• Good balance of evaluation and description, though it only becomes clear this is a PE lesson around two-thirds of the way through the evidence form, when some specific examples are given which will help when it comes to feedback to the teacher.

• The impact of the teaching on pupils' conduct and learning is reported clearly. There is reference to the focus of the observation, though this could be identified on the EF more clearly and be prioritised in the summary.

• The layout allows strengths and areas for improvement to be reported alongside each other, and the use of '–' signs help to identify AFI that will be helpful in feedback.

• Good information in the context box.

• Whether the judgement of a good lesson is accurate is debatable, taking into account the fact that only four or five of these overall above-average pupils showed secure technique by the end of the lesson. Does this represent good progress for these pupils? However, they all had a good knowledge of the technique and factors affecting the performance, and had secure evaluation skills. The weaknesses in health and safety are also factors affecting the overall judgement.

• Overall, rather long.

4. Evaluation and Feedback on the Lesson from the AST/Outreach Coordinator to the Class Teacher

Script

O = Observer
T = Teacher

The observer thanks the teacher.

O: *What part of the lesson did you enjoy most?*

T: *I enjoyed the warm-up skipping activities and the use of the ball for demonstrations.*
  Reasons for these are given.

O: *I agree, the strengths of the lesson were…*
  Observer states strengths of the lesson.

T: *I felt that there were weaknesses in…*
  Teacher explains where she felt there were weaknesses.

O: *Other strengths were that you had a good range of tasks. Pupils on the tasks were active and engaged. When seated, they were thinking. There were excellent expectations and demands on the students. You were also explicit about what you wanted them to achieve.*
  The observer feeds back strengths in assessment for learning, giving an example.
  The teacher replies but does not agree fully, stating why:

T: *Grace got to the triple jump and they were doing it with such fluency and covering such distance and maintaining such speed. Then I thought to myself, 'Hold on! They could be doing this much earlier in the lesson.' I think maybe, in retrospect, I could have spotted those sooner…'*

O: *There are two areas for development. The use of closed questions [gives an example]. Would you want to change the way they phrased those questions?*
  Discussion between the teacher and observer on the use of closed questions.

O: *The second area for development is progression of lesson. The progression did not follow a logical pattern.*
T: *Yes, I agree.*

O: *In summary, the strengths of the lesson and the areas for development are:*
  • *There was creative use of resources to include students and provide visual aids for students.*
  • *There was opportunity for pupil responsibility and autonomy.*
  • *Pupils were made responsible for their own learning and were encouraged to make decisions (eg estimating distances).*
  • *You made explicit demand for accuracy in student responses.*
  • *Your assessment for learning was very good.*
  Areas where you need to go further include:
  • *developing the range of questioning styles – especially at the start of the lessons*
  • *drawing out the cause and effect more.*

The observer gives judgements using the new Ofsted criteria.

O: *The lesson as a whole was a strong, good lesson.*

T: *Yes.*

O: *Learning: knowledge gains were good. Understanding was where the cause and effect comes in, where you need to take it next.*

Achievement: a strong good – it is a demanding skill to achieve differentiation of G&T children and catering for SEN was effective.

Attitudes and behaviour: they loved that lesson. You made effective use of praise. Teaching was good.

Good range of activities. Some more effective than others and you may want to alter that lesson in the light of activities that are more valuable.

Thanks again for your time and for allowing me to observe your lesson.

Evaluation of the Feedback

• The observer gives the teacher good opportunities to discuss features of the lesson and self-evaluate.

• There is a positive, professional atmosphere of trust and mutual respect.

• Strengths in teaching are clearly identified, although their impact on pupils' learning or achievement is not always made clear.

• The observer uses some good, specific examples to explain her judgements, including reference to her questioning of pupils.

• There is good reference to the focus of the observation (ie the development of thinking skills and use of a variety of approaches to suit pupils' different CAT profiles/learning styles).

• It is a good overall summary, marking clear strengths and areas for improvement.

• There are some inconsistencies in the evaluation of the quality of assessment for learning and too little challenge for higher-attaining pupils.

• Some weaknesses are not picked up (eg amount of sitting after the warm-up) and no reference to some health and safety issues (eg pit not raked often enough).

5. A Description of a Year 10 Class and Lesson Given by the AST

Outline of the Class

- 27 pupils – 11 girls and 16 boys.

- 7 G&T (2 for high CATs scores; 3 for science: 4 for PE practical).

- 6 SEN – 4 'Be aware'; 2 SA.

- Pupils at their target grades – overall above average.

Yellow sticker – verbal strength.
Green sticker – quantitative strength.
Pink sticker – non-verbal strength.
Blue sticker – even profile.

Script of the Pre-lesson Discussion Given by the AST

It's a Year 10 GCSE mixed-ability physical education class and it will be a theory lesson – so in a classroom. There are 27 pupils in total – 11 girls and 16 boys. There are seven Gifted and Talented pupils in the class: two of those have been flagged for CATs scores, three have been identified for science, which is specifically relevant to the content of the lesson today, and four have been specifically for their practical ability in PE itself. There are six SEN pupils: four at the 'Be aware' stage, two on SA stage, where they have IEPs to support their learning in lessons.

The most recent assessment point that went home had all, or the vast majority of students, working on or above their target grade.

In terms of identifying individual pupils within the lessons, you will be able to refer to the class list, where each student is numbered according to their alphabetical placement and their cognitive strength is recorded by colour, so those with a particular verbal strength will be wearing a yellow sticker, those with a quantitative strength will be wearing green, and non-verbal strength will be pink. And those who have an even profile, who are pretty similar across the cognitive abilities, will be wearing blue.

On the pupil name cards, the stickers will be there as well, so that in everyday lessons, students are aware themselves whether they have particular strength in one of the cognitive abilities.

As a school, we are looking towards doing something to extend that understanding for the students and for the members of staff themselves, so it forms effective differentiation in your classroom but also allows students to identify their strengths and use those to build on their weaker cognitive areas.

They are approximately halfway through the OCR GCSE physical education syllabus.

The lesson today is based on the skeleton. The actual module itself is called 'skeleton and joints'. In the past, I've taught those as separate entities, so I've done a couple of lessons on the skeleton and some on the joints and then some on muscles and, although it was effective, I did identify that students found it difficult to link the three together when talking about how the body moves, how it works. So, this time round, I've decided to put them all together and try that method so that straightaway, right from the word go, they can see the link.

By the end of the lesson, I would expect students to be able to identify major bones within the human body. I would expect that they understand why different types of bones exist and their related functions and jobs they do within the skeleton, and to be able to use this increased knowledge and this increased understanding to be able to answer set tasks such as an examination question that I've taken from a past paper, and also to be able to analyse the importance of the skeletal functions to a sport of their choice – to put it into a practical setting.

Q: So what are the key areas for the observer to focus on?

That's two-fold really. Like I say, my personal development is concentrated largely on the interpretation of CAT data and the CAT scores – how that can lead to effective differentiation both from a teacher point of view and a student independence to develop their own learning, but also a departmental focus that we have been working on for the past year now is developing higher-order thinking skills within the classroom, so that the pace and challenge of the lesson is at a much higher level.

Pupils							
Boys				**Girls**			
Number	Name	CAT Ability Profile	Target Grade	Number	Name	CAT Ability Profile	Target Grade
4	Nathan	Verbal	A	15	Jessica	Verbal	A
14	Rupert	Even?	B	5	Hannah C	Even	B
22	William	Even	B	13	Camilla		B
26	Russell	Verbal	B	19	Hannah R	Verbal	B
				21	Amy	Even	B
1	Dominic		C	24	Jenny	Verbal	C
3	Ryan	Quant.	C	27	Zoe		C
7	Steyel	Non-verbal	C	2	Sarah B		C
10	Chris		C	6	Amy C		C
11	John	Quant.	C	16	Jo P	Yellow?	C
23	Jamie	Non-verbal	C				
8	Jack	Non-verbal	D				
12	Jamie K	Verbal	D				
18	Sam P	Non-verbal	D				
20	Andrew	Non-verbal	D				
25	Oliver	Non-verbal	D				

Pupil number 4, Nathan, is above average.

Lesson Plan Year 10 GCSE Theory

Year group: 10	Week no: 1	Unit: *Skeleton and Joints*

Learning objectives – what you hope the students will learn:

• *Increase knowledge about the skeleton.*
• *Understand the importance of the skeleton for performance in sport.*
• *Use increased knowledge and understanding to answer set texts.*

Starter/introduction:

S. Bend elbow to bring arm across chest. Observe the back of your hand and forearm as you wiggle your fingers. Record what you see.
➤ *Collate arm information: bones/muscles/tendons/ligaments.*
Convert information into a diagram. (NV+ acts as a plan)
➤ *Flex/extend arm against force> feel bicep/tricep. What happens? Antagonistic pairs.*

Development (most):

• *Interpret and translate diagram to answer exam question: 'Explain and describe how physical movement takes place through the combined action of muscles and bones.' (3 marks) (NV+/V- record as a flow chart – fluency)*
• *Identify bones on skeleton w/sheet x 20.*
➤ *Recall individually, with partner, any one (diff colour). P. Textbook/poster.*
• *Bone classification (4 categories) same shape = same function.*
➤ *Examine skeleton carefully; decide on criteria for categories + 2 egs*
   (Clue; look for patterns/similarities in bone shape)
   a. Long, eg femur/radius – movement; investigate types of movement.
   Rubber band> 'long' long bone as levers/Pen exp. 'short' long bones for precision.
   b. Flat, eg pelvis/cranium – protection and large area for muscle attachment.
➤ *Decipher remaining functions and give eg > shape and support/blood production.*

Conclusion (plenary):

Analyse the importance of the functions of the skeleton to your chosen sport.
Organise answers according to cognitive strength; V+ paragraph/bullets, Q+ Flow chart, NV+ Mindmap.
Teacher and student assessment progress made over lesson.

Differentiation (all):

➤ *Writing frames, T/peer modelling + support clues, visual aids.*
Know more names of bones than did at start of lesson.
Describe at least one category of bone with an example and know its function.
Know the skeleton provides movement/protection and explain why important in a named sport.

Extension (some):

➤ *Use leg to answer Q, limited/adv support material.*
Know advanced terminology for names of bones.
Use the four categories of bone to explain the functions of the skeleton.
Able to discuss limitations of the skeleton and the need for additional protection in sport.

Grouping strategies:

Individual – student pairs (seating plan based on cognitive strengths).
Pair and share.
Whole class questioning and discussion.

Learning outcomes – assessing extent to which students have met learning objectives:

• *Identify specific bones in the human body.*
• *Understand why different types of bone exist and their different functions.*
• *Know the functions of the skeleton and analyse the importance of these to sport.*

Non-participants' role:	Language for learning:	
Notes.	Bone names	Antagonistic
➤ Short bones; carpals/tarsals – strength and movement in many directions.	Tendon	Lever
	Function	Precision
	Movement	Protection

Resources:		Health and fitness:
Textbooks	Posters	Context of the lesson – physical movement; skeletal framework.
Skeleton	Worksheets x 2	**Safety:**
Rubber band	Stickers	Movement around the classroom.

6. Year 10 GCSE Theory Lesson Taught by the AST

Time	Chapters and Lesson Activities
0 mins	Pupils find allotted seats; starter activity; teacher shares objectives and learning outcomes; pupils work with partners.
10 mins	Discussion and drawing of starter-activity findings; demo and discussion of arm anatomy; check of understanding etc.
20 mins	Review first objective; exam question set; teacher differentiates task for higher attainers and supports pupils.
30 mins	Poster shows answer to exam question; pupils work on next task to label as many bones in the skeleton as possible.
35 mins	Pupils collaborate on naming bones; pupils work in pairs to identify different categories of bones.
40 mins	Teacher leads class discussion on pupils' findings of different categories of bone and their functions.
50 mins	Class investigates how long bones in hand aid fine movement; teacher reviews second learning outcome.
55 mins	Discussion on how bones protect and enable movement in pupils' own sport; review of outcomes; new objectives shared.

Lesson Evidence Form

Evidence Form										
Inspector's OIN		Inspection number		Observation time		60		Observation type	L A D O	
Year group(s)	10	Grouping	**MC** SU SA SL O		BO GI **MI**			Present/NOR		
Subject codes	PE	Support teachers/ assistants	SEN / T / S	EAL / T / S	Oth / T / S	Inspector's EF No				

Focus (ie main purpose of the inspection activity):

How well used is CAT data to differentiate learning activities?

How effective is the teaching in developing pupils' thinking skills?

Context: *GCSE Theory*

Mixed-ability group: 7 x G&T (3 in SC, 4 in PE practical), 6 x SEN (2 x SA MLD, 4 x 'Be aware' stage). All on or above target grades. Overall above average ability. 77% A*–C. 2 x A, 7 x B, 12 x C, 5 x D.

L. Objectives *– increase knowledge of the skeleton – understand the importance of the skeleton for performance in sport – use increased K&U to answer set texts.*

L. Outcomes *– identify specific bones in the body – understand why different types of bone exist and their different functions – know the different functions of the skeleton and analyse the importance of these to sport.*

First lesson of new unit/module – 'Skeleton and Joints'. Covered modules on Fitness, Circulation, Respiration, Motivation.

Evaluation:

- *As a result of good relationships and high expectations, pupils work hard, have a go at tasks and are not afraid to make mistakes. They clearly enjoy the lessons.*

- *Pupils are clear on what they will learn and what is expected of them because the LOs are shared with them from the start of the lesson. The T refers to them throughout the lesson so that the pupils and the T can check on progress and set new targets. Overall assessment is contributing well to pupils' involvement, progress and learning.*

- *Not sure that pupils need to spend time writing out L objectives. Though this is clearly part of the lesson routine.*

- *Pupils are well motivated and involved in the lesson. They cooperate well in pairs and as a group. They respond well to the T's well-planned series of challenging tasks to find things out for themselves and each other.*

- *They readily use the skeleton and each other as resources to help them to learn. They are clearly used to working independently.*

- *The T's good K&U of individual pupils (CAT scores) helps her to suggest a variety of learning approaches to match individuals and to pose individually crafted questions.*

- *The variety of tasks, based on developing thinking skills, and their timing helped maintain a good pace to learning and pupils' interest. Planning clearly indicates a good range of 'thinking' that pupils will be engaged in, and tasks and questioning are generally successful so that pupils are identifying, recalling, classifying, examining and investigating.*

- *Less certain is whether pupils were successful in interpreting and translating what they knew well enough to be able to answer the exam question. Though this is to serve as a baseline task, it will be useful to return to this later in the module as a measure of success.*

- *The written task was not followed up fully, missing an opportunity to consolidate learning.*

- *Pupils are developing confidence in using the technical language because throughout the T draws attention to the terms, frequently checking pupils' understanding and using the WB well.*

- *The integrated approach being tried out appears to be helping to motivate pupils and help them see the relevance of K&U of bones and muscles.*

- *No use of ICT: missed opportunities to use PP and other interactive programmes.*

- *No homework given.*

- *Overall, pupils are making good progress and making appropriate gains in K&U. They are developing good independent learning skills and using a variety of ways of thinking.*

- *Plenary helped consolidate what had been learnt, though questioning could have demanded more evidence from the pupils of what they had learnt. Some questioning was closed.*

Evidence Form (continued)

Summary of main points:

Overall, a good lesson where pupils were challenged to think and work things out for themselves. A good variety of tasks helped maintain interest and pupils responded well to individual challenge and support given by the T, who knows the group very well. Overall, progress was good.

AFD

— *Make more use of ICT to support learning and teaching.*

— *Consider how best to support pupils in answering the set task (exam question) in applying their early, more limited K&U at this early stage in the unit, so that they are confident and benefit from the task.*

Judgement on the overall quality of the lesson (Leave blank when not a lesson) 1 = Outstanding, 4 = Inadequate	2

Use for grades if there is sufficient evidence:

Standards	Progress	Personal Development	Teaching	Curriculum	Care, Guidance and Support	Leadership and Management
	2	2	2			

Particular evaluations related to safety, health, enjoyment, contribution to the community and economic well-being:

Pupils enjoying the approaches to learning, where they are using a variety of thinking skills and taking responsibility for their own learning. Good focus on developing communication skills in terms of literacy and oral skills.

Evaluation of the Lesson Evidence Form

- Good balance of evaluation and description, though a few more specific examples would make sure that it is clear what subject is being taught.

- The impact of teaching on learning and learners is nearly always reported clearly.

- Good reference to the focus issues throughout the EF, though these could be highlighted more in the summary and they could be identified, perhaps with 'F' in the margins, to help pick them out easily to aid feedback and any summary a leader may be making of T&L against the focus issues. Plenty of relevant information in the context box.

- The grades reflect the text in the EF and this appears to be an accurate judgement of the lessons.

7. Evaluation and Feedback of the Year 10 GCSE Theory Lesson From the Head of PE to the AST

Script

O = Observer
T = Class teacher

O: *Right, before we start, just let's clarify the whole focus because I've really looked at it as a development lesson. I focused specifically on the thinking skills in GCSE because that's been part of our team improvement plan and I've really looked at the way you've used the CAT profiles, because you've been developing those in school anyway, but it's early days and I know that.*

T: *Yes, I know where I want to go with it but I haven't yet got there.*

O: *I wanted to talk about your learning objectives, and I wondered to what extent you think you have met them in this lesson.*

T: *If I look back, there are three separate ones but they all did tie in. I think that the first one was met by all students but at different levels. With the second one…but we still have to consolidate the link in terms with how that impacts on performance in sport. I think they can do it at a basic level, such as when playing rugby…but we definitely do need to take that forward, which is basically the final objective.*

O: *So, were you happy with the progress you made?*

T: *Yes, I was. They knew more than I thought they would know at certain points and, at other points, I thought they struggled to get to grips with what I wanted them to do. I didn't expect them to struggle at that particular point. It didn't come out how I expected it would. It was almost the reverse of that.*

O: *If you had a chance to do that again, is there one particular thing that you would change that would impact on making that lesson a little bit better?*

T: *It is difficult to answer that because the lesson formed a baseline assessment. I was surprised that they got the two functions of the skeleton as quickly as they did…I may not do an exam question or do a conditioned form. It did take up a lot of time and I felt it was left hanging. However, the group does need time to develop exam technique but it should not be the focus of the lesson.*

O: *Do you think in retrospect, because of the weakness you are highlighting, that you should not have put that in?*

T: *Yes, I do agree with that but then also it is my intention to give the same exam question again at the end of the module as a comparison.*

O: *Yes, this is a useful form of self-assessment.*

T: *There are other reasons for not including the exam question.*

The teacher explains reasons for an holistic approach.

The observer helps to justify the holistic approach as providing a range of different approaches and the things that need developing.

O: *The lesson plan. If we go to that first: the range of activities to match styles is a strong point of the lesson. From talking to students, this is common practice. You can handle a 'talking' class. It's very clear in the lesson plan that you are wanting to identify to yourself, so you are making sure that you are preparing for that with these thinking skills, so you've got words like 'convert', 'translate' and 'investigate'. I can see immediately that these are higher-order thinking skills identified. That's the first good thing that I can see, particularly because we have a GCSE group here. And the other thing, when I was looking through it, in terms of information you've given me about CAT scores, I don't personally think you can split the CAT scores and VAK, as they overlap. Good opportunity for different learning styles. There was good preparation for thinking skills – you've identified higher-order thinking skills.*

T: *There are a large number of non-verbal high-scoring/kinaesthetic learners, particularly among the boys.*

O: *If I can go on to some of the things that I think are really strong. You gave them good thinking time and created a safe environment for students to make mistakes in. You handled negative responses sensitively so that self-esteem was kept high. There was evidence that students felt comfortable making mistakes. You developed students' answers well. Good challenge to students, pushing students individually a little bit further.*

O: *Are you confident that most of those students were 'classifying' and 'interpreting'?*

T: *I am confident that the majority were successful with 'categorising' because of evidence from written and spoken work.*

O: *So you feel that you had enough evidence to support your assessment that they had used these HO skills?*

O: *So, if we go to some of the others, are there any there that you feel that you didn't get them to do?*

T: *Definitely, 'analyse'. But I think that we, as a group, are aware of that is something that we need to do. We know that is something we need to go back to.*

O: *What I want to do is now sum up the lesson. Basic strengths – some very nice things:*

- *There was clarity in the objectives – students were well rehearsed in getting those objectives down.*
- *I like the way they use each other as experts and touch things and look things up in books.*
- *There is a lot of thinking going on [O gives a good example].*
- *You did try to get students to work independently – good for lifelong learning.*
- *There was a secure environment where it was OK to make mistakes – builds their self-esteem.*

You had tried today to really look at how to use CAT profiles. You would agree there is still a long way to go [T agrees], but you have made a real positive start today in trying to break that down and analyse that. In terms of further development, I think I would say to you that you have got to carry on with work in terms of exploring, using and maximising CAT profiles. I do think that you need to perhaps consider the VAK work and revisit it and see if there is any overlap between the CAT profiling, because you might not have to redesign the wheel. So, having said that, with some concerns about the attainment of some of the pupils, attitudes and behaviour were excellent, learning was good, the achievement was good and the teaching was good – the attainment was good. There was a little bit of confusion. I'm happy to say that was a very strong, good lesson.

The observer refers to Ofsted criteria to justify the good grade and encourages the teacher.

O: *I think that is a super start. So, thanks very much.*

T: *Thank you.*

Evaluation of Feedback

• Very clear overall judgements.

• Well-focused observation and feedback.

• The observer gives the teacher plenty of opportunity for reflection and self-analysis.

• Good level of professional discussion.

• Some parts of the feedback do not make explicit links between teaching and the outcomes for pupils.

Appendix III: Example of a Completed SEF from Biddick School

Who and What is the Form For?

This self-evaluation form (SEF) is a summative document, intended to record the outcomes of your ongoing process of rigorous self-evaluation[5]. The self-evaluation form will also be used to inform:

- your improvement plan

- SMT-led evaluations

- the whole-school self-evaluation form (SEF)

- a whole-school Ofsted inspection

- a subject or thematic Ofsted inspection.

As such, it should be an accurate diagnostic document, with all conclusions fully supported by the evidence. It should indicate key strengths and weaknesses, and what needs to be tackled to effect improvement. The impact of your self-evaluation in helping to bring about improvement will be a major factor in any judgements about the effectiveness of your leadership and management, and your capacity to improve in the future.

When Do You Complete the Self-evaluation Form?

- This form should be completed by the department using the training day to complete the sections on personal development and well-being (4a–4e). You will have copies of all other curriculum areas to support you.

- Our whole-school SEF will be sent to you for the start of the new school year.

- The training day will further support the writing of the SEF, with time in departments.

- Conclusions from your meetings with your team, and to review this summer's GCSE and SATs data, will be important.

- **This form should be updated throughout the year** as new evidence emerges from your self-evaluation process. New evidence could, for example, materialise from performance data, assessments, records of learners' progress, pupil or parent surveys, lesson observations, scrutiny of pupils' work, pupil discussions, reviews or inspections, improvement planning etc.

General Advice for Completing this Self-evaluation Form

The more self-evaluation was based on honest assessment of the school's strengths and weaknesses, the easier the inspectors found it to focus the inspection sharply.

'A New Relationship with Schools: Improving Performance through School Self-evaluation' (DfES, 2004)

The qualities Ofsted expect to see in an SEF are:

- **honesty**

- **accuracy**

- **rigour.**

[5] A working group of curriculum leaders and senior management will be meeting during the summer term to review or present self-evaluation processes. One outcome will be an annual cycle linking self-evaluation and improvement planning.

The following points will help:

- Keep it simple and avoid jargon.
- Try to be accurate and clear.
- Prioritise – describe future goals and how they might be achieved.
- Answer the questions by making clear judgements and remember each time to justify answers with a brief summary of the evidence.
- Evidence must be robust. Assertion is not good enough. For instance, refer briefly to test and examination results where data is available and reliable, but remember to say what the data told you, prompted you to do, and the impact of your actions.
- When making judgements, link cause and effect.
- Refer to other reliable evidence where it is relevant. It is not intended that there should be large amounts of data and descriptive detail, and evidence should be used selectively to support judgements. You can indicate clearly in the SEF where more detailed evidence can be found.
- Remember to comment, not just on what you have done to promote the outcomes, but also on the **impact** that this has had on learners. You should always try to comment on the difference that your action has made to particular groups of learners in relation to their progress.
- Once completed, your SEF should reflect your link SMT and governors' involvement in your self-evaluation, and show that it has been completed with their agreement.

Documents Relevant to the Completion of the Self-evaluation Form

The following can be obtained in hard copy from the Ofsted website (www.ofsted.gov.uk) or from the schools' Intranet.

- 'Every Child Matters: Framework for the Inspection of Schools in England from September 2005' (Ofsted, 2005).
- 'Guidance for Inspectors of Schools: Using the Evaluation Schedule' (Ofsted, 2005).
- 'Guidance for Inspectors of Schools: Conducting the Inspection' (Ofsted, 2005).
- 'A New Relationship with Schools: Improving Performance through School Self-evaluation' (Ofsted, 2005).
- A blank Ofsted secondary SEF.

How to Fill Your Form In

The self-evaluation form is laid out in sections that correspond to the headings of the evaluation schedule in the 'Framework for the Inspection of Schools', although overall effectiveness and efficiency are placed last in the SEF (Section 7).

Please complete first the sections dealing with Achievement and Standards (3) and Personal Development and Well-being (4), since these outcomes will form the basis for your judgements in other sections.

Reference is made to the 'Guidance for Inspectors of Schools'. This guidance is in two parts. One relates to the use of the evaluation schedule, which contains advice on how to pitch judgements about the quality of provision and its outcomes. The other is guidance on conducting the inspection, which should also prove helpful to you since it indicates how aspects of your area might be explored by inspectors.

Each section of the SEF asks you to grade aspects of your work on a four-point scale, as follows:

Grade 1: Outstanding

Grade 2: Good

Grade 3: Satisfactory

Grade 4: Inadequate.

The grade descriptions in the 'Guidance for Inspectors of Schools' will assist you to reach accurate judgements. It is most important that you complete this form rigorously and objectively.

When completing the text boxes, you should summarise your main findings and illustrate with the evidence that led to the judgements being made, bearing in mind the specific questions written in each of the boxes. It is not intended that you should provide large amounts of statistical data and descriptive detail. You should use evidence selectively to support the main judgements about your performance.

Self-evaluation Form (SEF) for Curriculum Leaders

1. Characteristics of Your Curriculum Area or Area of Responsibility

What are the main characteristics of your curriculum area or area of responsibility?

This is an opportunity for a **brief summary** of the main characteristics of your area and it is not necessary to repeat tables of data from other parts of the SEF. You may wish to draw on Sections B and C of the whole-school SEF.

1a Please outline the main characteristics of the learners

- Remember: you are writing about the characteristics of your learners, **not** what you do to support them.

- In this section, you should identify:
  – attainment on entry in Year 7 and how you know this
  – attainment on entry to Key Stage 4.

- Break down groups of learners and their particular needs, identifying any particular aids or barriers to achievement (which you intend to write in more detail in Section 3: Achievement and Standards).

- Identify those who perform better or less well than the school's main group.

- Identify how your area strives to include all vulnerable groups (eg ethnic minorities, English as an additional language, looked-after and disaffected children).

- Include, as relevant, any significant changes in cohorts or turbulence factors and their impact.

- Refer to the importance of seeking the views of stakeholders to ensure that your perception is accurate.

NB Any assertion must be supported by evidence. For example:

- Attainment on entry in Year 7 is in line with national expectations – NC levels from feeder schools and baseline assessments carried out by PE staff after first half-term.

- Attainment on entry to Key Stage 4 – 99% of students at NC level 5 or above.

1b Please summarise briefly your distinctive aims and describe any special features of your area

For example:

- Your area's mission statement, main vision or purpose – how this is agreed and shared, particularly with stakeholders.

- Evidence of stability of staff, strong leadership and effective evaluation of activities.

- Identify the **impact** of any particular status or specific initiatives/projects – specialist school, EiC (G&T, Learning Mentors, Aim Higher), New Opportunities Funding, Key Stage 3 strategies, healthy schools, development of our sixth form provision, primary links, international links, community links, extended provision etc.

- Significant partnerships with other providers or agencies (such as shared arrangements for the curriculum, federal arrangements or partnerships with employers).

This provides you with the opportunity to express what you believe to be the underlying ethos and purpose of your area. Listing your intentions without describing the underlying principles and values that underpin these actions is not enough. Whatever you say in this section must have a resonance throughout the rest of the document.

PE Department:

- Sports College status since 1998.

- 'Sportsmark Gold' redesignated 2004.

- Hard-working, supportive teaching team with a large number of highly experienced staff, a number of whom have been at Biddick School Sports College for 10 years or more.

- Expertise in a wide range of activities and styles of teaching.

- High standards of behaviour and performance expected from all students.

- Promotion of lifelong participation in healthy physical activity.

- Good relationships between staff and students.

- Pupil progress is very good.

- Mixed-ability groupings.

- Majority of students take a pride in their ability to perform well in the subject and enjoy their lessons.

- Enjoyment of lessons seen to be of equal importance to high-quality teaching and learning.

- Broad and balanced curriculum.

- Staff are encouraged to observe each other in order to develop their expertise in all areas of the curriculum.

- Staff demonstrate the flexibility to cope with environmental conditions and staff absence.

- Students are encouraged to take ownership of their own learning – leading warm-up, teaching each other, refereeing, JSLA, etc.

- Opportunities to experience 'off-site' activities.

- Wide range of competitive and non-competitive extra-curricular activities as well as inter-form/school competitions available.

- Opportunities for talented students to gain representative honours in a wide range of sports.

- Opportunities for academically lower-ability students to be seen as high achievers in this subject.

- Success is celebrated at whatever level it is achieved – sports awards evening, presentation evenings.

- Staff are keen to develop their teaching skills in order to enhance provision for our students.

- Opportunities for students who have left to continue their involvement with the department/school.

- PE staff delivering INSET at Sunderland Schools' PE and Sport conference/leading sessions at YST area subject leaders' meetings and national Sports Colleges' Conference.

Impact of Sports College status:

- High-quality staff employed by the school.

- Access to cutting edge INSET/staff development (eg Sports Colleges Conference).

- Opportunity to undertake research projects.

- International links developed – Russia, China, Poland – 'Dreams and Teams'.

- Funding for school minibuses to enhance extra-curricular provision.

- Expanded range of extra-curricular opportunities (eg climbing, skiing).

- Funding for purchase of equipment (eg Dartfish ICT package, coaching support, and enhancement of Key Stage 4 curriculum).

- Funding to support GCSE PE OAA weekend in the Lake District – raising standards achieved in this activity area and, therefore, raising overall GCSE PE attainment levels.

- Links with feeder schools created – PE support teacher in feeder schools – raising standards of teaching and learning.

- Improved links with partner secondary schools.

- School/club links developed – gymnastics, basketball, netball, rugby, tennis.

- Teacher/Coach Education Centre in partnership with Human Kinetics and NGBs established.

- Federation – links with other City of Sunderland sports colleges created – raising standards of teaching and learning across the City of Sunderland.

- Access to NOF3 funding for new buildings and refurbishing of other facilities.

- Purchase of corporate staff clothing and team kits.

Impact of NOF funding:

- New changing facilities – will enhance pride in Biddick and promote positive attitudes to PE lessons.

- Fitness centre – will allow department to monitor students' levels of fitness and increase awareness of a variety of training methods to support GCSE PE work.

- Coach Education Centre – will enhance coaching/teaching provision across the City of Sunderland by allowing access to the latest information/teaching aids.

- Allows the opportunity to deliver A-level and higher level BTEC courses on site.

1c Please outline specific contextual or other issues that act as aids or barriers to raising performance (for each, refer to impact on attainment)

The danger in this section is the temptation to focus upon those factors acting as potential or actual barriers to learning and, while these have to be acknowledged, it is also important to note those factors that aid progress or have the potential to do so. The aim must be not to give the impression of an excuse culture existing within an area.

You could include references to:

- Attainment on entry at each phase – how this impacts overall.

- Levels of need, including vulnerable groups, and the implications for provision in meeting these needs.

It may be helpful to think of this in terms of:

- resources: aids and barriers – buildings, people, equipment

- training: aids and barriers

- community: local factors that aid or impinge on learning (eg parental aspirations; youth culture).

Some examples include:

Primary and post-16 transfer and transition projects; whole-school and departmental CPD; new teachers' group; school improvement group; leadership courses; involvement in local or national network learning; advanced skills teachers; cluster projects; master classes; departmental and business mentoring; corrective reading and numeracy; university support; G&T and learning mentor initiatives; strategies for groups of learners (SEN, underachievers, G&T etc); governor involvement; recent changes of leadership.

Aids to raising performance:

- Advanced Skills Teacher – Dance – raising standards of teaching and learning in this area in feeder schools and at GCSE level. PE department SIG representative developing resources to aid Assessment for Learning in PE lessons.

- Pilot school for AQA Applied GCSE in Physical Education.

- Tennis, basketball, gymnastics and netball master classes delivered on site for pupils from feeder schools and Biddick School.

- Multi-skills academy based at Biddick School attended by G&T pupils from feeder schools.

- Excellent facilities for delivery of the subject.

- Teacher/Coach Education Centre giving all teachers/coaches in the City of Sunderland access to up-to-date information/lesson planning and delivery materials.

Barriers to raising performance:

- Sports hall unavailable for all of autumn term 2005 – impact on curriculum and extra-curricular provision.

- Poor standard of changing facilities for all of autumn term 2005 – negative impact on pupils' behaviour at beginning and end of PE lessons.

- A number of PE staff are unable to drive the minibuses – restrictions on some extra-curricular activities.

- Bad weather has a considerable impact on the curriculum at times throughout the year.

1d Please note any additional characteristics of your area that you would particularly like to draw attention to

This is an opportunity to describe what you believe to be unique or unusual features of your area, but it is imperative that it is related to learners' outcomes. Examples include:

• strengths in your curriculum – enrichment focus.

• innovative practice – teaching and learning, action research, timetabling.

• national or local initiative involvement – pilot projects.

Strengths:

• Standard of teaching and learning – lesson observation, SMT departmental review 2003, GCSE PE results.

• Key Stage 4 curriculum – high rates of participation – lesson registers.

• Extra-curricular provision – wide range of opportunities available.

Innovative practice:

• Action research – the effectiveness of the Basic Moves programme in raising standards of practical performance.

• Action research – the effectiveness of the use of SAQ drills and equipment in raising standards of practical performance.

• Developing the use of ICT in PE lessons – video analysis, CD-ROM, Edexcel revision package.

• Developing and evaluating resources for AQA Applied GCSE – Physical Education.

National/local initiative involvement:

• Involvement in the delivery of A-level and BTEC courses in conjunction with the shared sixth form at college.

• Pilot school for AQA Applied GCSE – Physical Education.

• Delivery of Basic Moves programme in feeder schools.

1e Please outline briefly the main priorities in your improvement/development plan, and how they reflect the context in which you work

This is to assess whether your area of the school knows itself well and has prioritised appropriately in the light of its strengths and weaknesses and unique context. This section allows you to draw this together and, like section 1b: Summarise Briefly your Distinctive Aims and Describe any Special Features of Your Area, it should be reflected in other relevant sections of the SEF.

Includes:

• the main features of your improvement plan (Ofsted expects to see a single plan to assess whether the school and each aspect has accurately identified its priorities)

• a bullet-point summary of this section. A general evaluative comment is welcomed here to round up the section (eg 'Our evidence base demonstrates the success of practice to date but we are not complacent and strive to achieve even higher').

- Review of programmes of study to reflect increased attainment at the end of Key Stage 2.

- Improved teaching and learning through the development of Assessment for Learning (Key Stage 3 Strategy).

- Improved performance in written exams at GCSE level in PE and in Dance through enhanced ICT provision and further development of teaching materials and resources.

- Development of programme of study for AQA Vocational GCSE in PE.

- Development of teaching and learning links (kinaesthetic learning) between sport and science.

2. Views of Learners, Parents/Carers and Other Stakeholders

What are the views of learners, parents/carers and other stakeholders and how do you know?

The charts overleaf help you identify the stakeholders whom we are likely to consult as a school. Some of this will be done centrally and the outcomes passed on to you. You could use this table as an aide-memoire prior to completing this section of the SEF. Its completion will help you identify the type of contact made with each group: when, how often, and how these views are shared with others.

The last chart on page 164 overleaf allows you to go into further detail by recording for each major stakeholder group, not just how they are consulted, but also what information their views have provided for the school, how the school or your area has gone back and shared these findings with stakeholders, and what actions have been taken in response to the views expressed.

Chart recording the ways in which the views of stakeholders can be gathered and how these views are shared with the wider community. *NB Spaces have been left for you to add your own.*			
Type of contact	**Frequency**	**Timing**	**2c: How do you share?**
Governors			
Governor visits			
Sub-committee meetings			
Full governor meetings			
Questionnaire			
Contribution to annual report (profile)			
Parents/carers			
Parents evenings			
Questionnaires			
Surgeries			
Complaints procedures			
Working party on ( )			
PTA feedback			
Comments on reading records			

Chart recording the ways in which the views of stakeholders can be gathered and how these views are shared with the wider community. NB *Spaces have been left for you to add your own.*			
Type of contact	**Frequency**	**Timing**	**2c: How do you share?**
Learners			
School-council minutes			
During class observations			
Pupil interviews – subject monitoring			
Informal (ad hoc)			
Pupil attitude survey			
Healthy schools audit			
MIDYIS/YELLIS/ALIS			
School staff			
Staff meetings			
Performance-management interviews			
360° review of leadership team			
Confidential questionnaire			

Community groups			
Groups using the building questionnaire			
Community association			
Neighbours			
Local council			
Business/school partnership			
Family of schools			
Specialist school steering committee			
APPGs			
External agencies			
Link adviser			
School nurse			
ESW			
Ofsted			
Social Services			
IIP			

Gathering the Views of Learners, Parents/Carers and Other Stakeholders

Group:				
Evidence base			**2b**	**What do their views tell you about: standards, personal development and well-being, and the quality of your provision?**
Type of contact	**Frequency**	**Timing**		
2d Give examples of actions taken based upon the views of ( ), with an evaluation of the effectiveness of what you did.		**2c How do you share your findings with stakeholders?**		

2a How do you gather the views of learners, parents/carers and other stakeholders, such as those accessing additional services, how often do you do this, and how do you ensure the impartiality of the information?

2b What do the views of learners, parents/carers and other stakeholders tell you about the learners' standards, personal development and well-being, and the quality of your provision?

2c How do you share with parents/carers and other stakeholders the collated findings about their views?

2d Can you give examples of action you have taken based on the views of learners, parents/carers or other stakeholders, with an evaluation of the effectiveness of what you did?

• Are there examples of actions you decided not to take (with the reasons for this)?

• Are there examples of ways in which your stakeholders have influenced the priorities noted in section 1e. The main priorities in your improvement/development plan? (Please cross-refer to any relevant comments in the leadership and management section.)

3. Achievement and Standards

How well do learners achieve?

To help you focus your comment and judgements in completing this section, please consult the relevant pages in the 'Guidance for Inspectors of Schools'.

3a What are learners' achievements and standards in their work?

- The **standards** learners reach as indicated by their test and examination results, taking account of: any significant variations between groups of learners, subjects, courses and key stages; trends over time; comparisons with other schools; whether learners reach challenging targets – the **standards** of learners' **current work** in relation to their learning goals (noting any significant differences between current work and recent results).

- Learners' **progress** relative to their starting points and capabilities, with any significant variations between groups of learners (**making clear whether there are any groups that are underachieving and could be doing better**).

1. Present Key Performance Outcomes	2. Evidence Base
• End of KS 3 NC levels are well above national levels: NC5+ 2003 – 98%, 2004 – 98%, 2005 – 99%.	• PANDA information and department records
• End of KS 4 NC levels: NC7+ 2003 – 74%. High conversion rate between levels at end of KS 3 and 4.	• PANDA information and department records
• GCSE Physical Education results have exceeded targets for four out of the last five years. Pupils' average points score is higher than the average in all their other subjects for the past five years, and the Relative Performance Indicator for this period is significantly positive each year.	• Department assessment records • GCSE results and PANDA information
• In 2004 and 2005, all teachers of GCSE PE have had positive residuals when results are compared with YELLIS and MAG predictions.	• GCSE results analysis
• GCSE PE A*/C: 2003 – 49%, 2004 – 75%, 2005 – 67%.	• GCSE results
• GCSE Dance results A*/C: 2003 – 0%, 2004 – 60%, 2005 – 23%.	• GCSE results

3. Summary of Strengths and Weaknesses

Strengths
- High standards of teaching and learning.
- End of Key Stage National Curriculum levels and conversion rate between levels.
- Individual assessments at the end of each block of work.
- Almost all students achieve a NC level commensurate with, or above, what is expected for their age.
- GCSE Physical Education results.
- Value-added information at GCSE.
- Results from inter-school competitions across a wide range of activities.

Weaknesses
- Students need to be more aware of what they must improve in order to achieve the next level in each activity area.
- Written examination performance in GCSE PE and Dance.
- Number of A* grades achieved at GCSE level.
- Current programmes of study may not take account of improved standards of performance at Key Stage 2.

4. Actions Already Taken to Improve
- Teachers have high expectations of their pupils with regard to behaviour, attitude and performance.
- Increased use of ICT in GCSE theory lessons to improve student engagement and motivation in this area.
- Challenging pupil-progress performance-management targets set.
- Development of girls' curriculum at KS 3 to include fitness activities, dance and football.
- Update of basketball and hockey programmes of study.

5. Future Targets
(Learning Outcomes)
- Students are aware of their targets for improvement of their performance in each activity area.
- Improve average written exam performance in GCSE PE to 75/150 and in GCSE Dance to 50/100.
- Increase the number of students achieving A* grades in GCSE PE by 50%.
- Football and netball programmes of study updated.

6. Future Actions to Achieve Targets
- Development of resources for Assessment for Learning.
- Continue to increase access to ICT in GCSE theory lessons by accessing teaching facility in NOF3 building project.
- Additional mock exam to be taken.
- New GCSE PE workbooks to be developed so that students have a high-quality revision tool.
- PE mentors appointed to Year 11 students identified as possible A* candidates.
- Extra coaching sessions in practical areas to take place during February half-term and Easter holiday.
- Review of football and netball programmes of study.

Please enter grades. To guide judgement, please consult grade descriptions in the 'Guidance for Inspectors of Schools'.

	Outstanding	Good	Satisfactory	Inadequate
Learners' achievement and standards in their work		**X**		

An Example Reflecting a Whole School SEF

1. Present Key Performance Outcomes	2. Evidence Base
Most learners attain high standards and achieve better-than-expected progress across the school: • In relation to schools nationally, learners achieve well above expected (B) except in English (C) (particularly writing), where a number of middle-ability boys are known to underachieve. • In relation to similar schools (FSM), learners achieve above average (B), except in English (C). Learners achieve their targets, based on KS2/FFT data. • Higher attainers do very well and make better-than-expected progress in Year 9 (L6/7 – A). Others subjects are at least satisfactory. Learners achieve very well in ICT, the arts and PE.	School's analysis of tests at end of key stages (1). • LEA data (2). • Optional tests/TAs (3). • Progress of cohorts by key-stage average points (4). • Individual tracking, progress of vulnerable group of middle-ability boys (5). • KS 2–KS 3 (6). • PANDA analysis (7). • MIDYIS (8). • LEA monitoring – standards summary (9). • FFT data (10). • Learners' views (11). • Lesson observations (12).

3. Summary of Strengths and Weaknesses

Strengths

- Majority of learners achieve standards above those nationally/similar schools. Teaching is strong and learners make 4+ points progress over a year (4, 5, 12).
- Overall, all groups perform well. Progress is sound across other subjects/courses, with learners making good progress in a number of areas (2, 3).
- Challenging targets are set for the end of each year and learners know what they need to do to achieve (3).
- Learners are regularly consulted and feel they are supported well (11, 12).

Weaknesses

- A small number of middle-ability boys make less progress than they should, particularly in Year 8 (5).
- In D+T and MFL, where the curriculum is less well developed and recruitment remains difficult, progress is satisfactory.

4. Actions Already Taken to Improve

- Adoption/development/commitment to effectively embrace KS 3 strategy materials across all subjects.
- Staff have ownership of data – know what is expected.
- Expectation is high – pace in lessons.
- Staff PM targets – challenging – linked to attainment of specific group/subject.
- Whole staff INSET – consistent messages.

5. Future Targets

(Learning Outcomes)

- Learners make consistent progress across the school/key stage (1, 2, 5, 6, 7, 8).
- Progress of average achievers (boys) in English in Years 7 and 8 monitored termly – 10% improvement expected over current year (4, 5).
- In D+T and MFL, external curriculum support enables learners to develop better skills, and tracking indicates that a significant number make better-than-expected progress (3).
- High attainers continue to achieve better-than-average results (1, 2, 4, 7, 9, 10).

6. Future Actions to Achieve Targets

- Intervention strategies targeted at group of middle-achieving boys in English. Additional teaching and support staff deployed to Year 8, where least progress is made.
- Enhance provision in D+T and MFL, part-support built in to allow more learners to study and to enrich curriculum. Provide CPD for current staff.
- Set challenging target for incoming Year 7, particularly middle achievers (boys) and track termly to identify/intervene early.

4. Personal Development and Well-being

How good is the overall personal development and well-being of the learners?

To help you focus your comment and judgements in completing this section, please consult the relevant pages in the 'Guidance for Inspectors of Schools'. In answering the following questions, please make clear the main evidence on which your evaluation is based.

4a How does your curriculum area contribute to learners adopting healthy lifestyles?

• Whether learners take adequate physical exercise and eat and drink healthily.

• Learners' growing understanding of how to live a healthy lifestyle.

1. Present Key Performance Outcomes	2. Evidence Base
• Two-and-a-half hours of Physical Education per week for students in Years 7 and 8. • Two hours of Physical Education per week for students in Years 9, 10 and 11. • Additional two hours per week for Year 10 and 11 students who opt for GCSE PE or Dance. • Additional four hours per week for Year 10 and 11 students who opt for BTEC Sport. • Sportsmark Gold Award and FA Charter Mark. • Health and hygiene talk – Year 7 and Year 10 girls – improved awareness and increased participation in lessons. • High-quality teaching in the subject area motivates students to take part in curricular and extra-curricular activities. • Coaching support in lesson delivery – staff development which leads to improved quality of teaching and learning.	• Timetable/curriculum manager. • Award certificates. • Pupil interview and class registers. • Class registers and extra-curricular participation records. • Lesson observation.

3. Summary of Strengths and Weaknesses

Strengths

• Time set aside for Physical Education lessons.

• Excellent facilities for Physical Education.

• Attendance at extra-curricular Physical Education activities.

• Students are encouraged to take responsibility for their own learning – leading warm-up, leadership programmes, fitness activities.

• High levels of participation in Physical Education lessons.

• GCSE PE theory work on health and fitness issues – use of drugs, diet, smoking, hygiene, etc.

Weaknesses

• Lack of facilities for fitness training work at Key Stage 4.

4. Actions Already Taken to Improve

• Development of GCSE PowerPoint presentations on health and fitness issues.

• Provision of a fitness suite as part of the NOF3 building programme.

5. Future Targets

(Learning Outcomes)

• Students at Key Stage 4 will develop their knowledge and understanding of health and fitness issues through the use of equipment in the fitness suite.

• Investigate extra-curricular areas for further development in order to increase participation, particularly at lunchtime.

6. Future Actions to Achieve Targets

• All Year 10 students will complete a block of work in the fitness suite.

• Year 11 students will be able to select a fitness training option that will be based in the fitness suite.

• 'Healthy Lifestyle' display.

• Student survey/questionnaire.

An Example Reflecting a Whole School SEF

To what extent do learners adopt healthy lifestyles?

1. Present Key Performance Outcomes • Vast majority of pupils attending school take part in two hours' PE every week. • Many children take part in clubs during the week. • There is an emerging recognition by the children of healthy eating and drinking, and their actions are changing accordingly. • Increasing numbers of pupils are requesting healthier food choices. • Most of our children demonstrate good levels of self-esteem.	**2. Evidence Base** **Direct observation** • Class lessons (1). • Lunchtime supervision (2). • School trips (3). **Testimony** • Staff-meeting feedback (4). • School council (5). • Annual parent questionnaire (6). **Data/evidence** • Pupil attitude survey (7). • Healthy schools audit (8). • Clubs registers (9). • PE registers (10). • Healthy eating policy (11).
3. Summary of Strengths and Weaknesses **Strengths** • Participation in physical activities and enjoyment of these is a real strength (1, 2, 3, 9, 10). • There is an emerging realisation of healthy eating and drinking (1, 2, 4, 5, 7). • High level of pupil self-esteem demonstrated in their confident, outgoing manner (1, 5, 7, 8). **Weaknesses** • Though active at school, too many learners lead a sedentary lifestyle at home (7, 6). • There is an ignorance of the dangers and benefits of drugs (1, 8). • The body hygiene of a significant number of children is a problem (1).	**4. Actions Already Taken to Improve** CPD/Resource deployment/ Policies/Teaching • Major focus on healthy eating (11). • Developed a Healthy Learner Charter (11). • Programme of extended school activities (9).

5. Future Targets	6. Future Actions to Achieve Targets
(Learning Outcomes)	
• Vast majority of pupils (90%) will, by June 2007, have an age-appropriate understanding of and response to the dangers and benefits of drugs. • Large majority of children will be demonstrating much more physically active lifestyles out of school.	• Drug-awareness training of staff and parents. • Drug-awareness policy rewritten with the children. • Increase opportunities for and awareness of healthy lifestyle options after school.

4b How does your curriculum area contribute to learners feeling safe and adopting safe practices?

• Whether learners feel safe from bullying and racist incidents.

• The extent to which learners have the confidence to talk to staff and others when they feel at risk.

1. Present Key Performance Outcomes	2. Evidence Base
• Teachers expect that students demonstrate positive attitudes while in the subject area – enthusiasm, encouragement of one another and high rates of participation evident in every lesson. • Students enjoy their PE lessons. • Safe working practices mean that there are relatively few injuries in PE lessons and first-aid assistance is always on hand. • Allowances made for individual circumstances, eg PE kit, highlighting success at all levels of ability, alterations made to an individual's curriculum as appropriate. • Involvement in 'Show Racism the Red Card' initiative – increased knowledge and awareness of racism in sport/racist attitudes.	• Lesson observation and class registers. • Effort grades and positive comments in annual reports to parents. • Few incidents in the PE department have to be dealt with by the SMT. • Pupil interview and participation records. • Accident forms and first-aid certificates. • Lesson observation and pupil interview. • Work produced in English department.

3. Summary of Strengths and Weaknesses

Strengths

- Teaching staff all have excellent subject knowledge and have high expectations of their pupils with regard to their behaviour and attitude.

- Three members of the department are currently qualified first-aiders.

- 'Fair play', positive feedback and constructive criticism are all encouraged. Inappropriate or unacceptable behaviour is dealt with immediately. This leads to a positive working atmosphere for all.

Weaknesses

- Poor-quality changing facilities – overcrowding can lead to some pupils feeling uncomfortable at the start and end of lessons.

4. Actions Already Taken to Improve

- Risk assessments carried out for all activities covered in the PE curriculum.

- NOF3 building programme will provide large, high-quality changing areas for indoor and outdoor PE lessons.

- BSkyB programme aimed at increasing pupil self-esteem.

5. Future Targets
(Learning Outcomes)

- Help G&T students to manage their time more effectively and promote positive relationships between parents/pupils/teachers/coaches.

6. Future Actions to Achieve Targets

- Sports mentoring and JAE programmes implemented.

4c How much do learners enjoy their education in your curriculum area?

• Take account of learners' attitudes, behaviour and attendance.

• Learners' spiritual, moral, social, emotional and cultural development.

1. Present Key Performance Outcomes	2. Evidence Base
• High participation levels and wearing correct kit for PE. • Effort grades, comments on positive attitudes in annual reports to parents. • Students' commitment to extra-curricular clubs. • Good relationships between staff and students. • High-quality teaching in the subject area motivates students to participate in curricular and extra-curricular activities.	• Class registers and lesson observation. • Copy reports. • Attendance records – extra-curricular clubs. • Data from school questionnaires. • Lesson observation.
3. Summary of Strengths and Weaknesses **Strengths** • Example set by staff and their insistence on high standards of behaviour. • Students' support and encouragement of each other. • Group work – mixed-gender lessons – celebration and appreciation of success. • Development of a sense of fair play and appreciation of high standards of performance by oneself and other people. **Weaknesses** • Small number of students in each year group whose participation record in PE is poor.	4. Actions Already Taken to Improve • Celebration of success in assemblies. • Presentation evenings/Sports awards evening.
5. Future Targets (Learning Outcomes) • All students will take part in PE lessons unless they have an injury or illness which prevents them from doing so.	6. Future Actions to Achieve Targets • Close monitoring of participation records by head of department. • Liaison with parents when a student has problems with participation. • Spare PE kit available for any student who forgets their kit.

4d How does your curriculum area contribute to learners making a positive contribution to the community?

- Learners' growing understanding of their rights and responsibilities, and of those of others.
- How well learners express their views and take part in communal activities.

1. Present Key Performance Outcomes

- School/club links – basketball, netball, gymnastics, rugby.
- Organisation of Sports Leaders courses – 'Dreams and Teams' – organisation of sports festivals.
- Dance performances.
- Involvement in 'Show Racism the Red Card' initiative – increased knowledge and awareness of racism in sport/racist attitudes.
- Residential trips – ski trip, Derwent Hill outdoor centre – students gain the skills and the awareness to continue with these activities.

2. Evidence Base

- Clubs' participation records.
- Sports Leaders record books and student exchange links with Poland.
- Video evidence and pupil interview.
- Work produced in English department.
- Pupil interview.

3. Summary of Strengths and Weaknesses

Strengths

- School/club links – many students have developed the skills and the confidence to attend a wide variety of sports clubs in the community.
- Sports Leadership – exchange links with Poland, organisation of junior school sports festivals.
- Year 11 'off-site' options programme – increases students' awareness of opportunities to take part in sport in the community.
- Dance performances (eg International Kite Festival) – students gain experience of performing in public.

Weaknesses

4. Actions Already Taken to Improve

- Continued development of Year 11 'off-site' programme – climbing lessons and climbing club set up.
- Sports Leaders supporting PE staff in lessons with junior school pupils.

5. Future Targets
(Learning Outcomes)

6. Future Actions to Achieve Targets

4e How does your curriculum area contribute to learners preparing for their future economic well-being?

- How well learners develop skills and personal qualities that will enable them to achieve future economic well-being.
- Learners' understanding of career options and the acquisition of workplace skills.

1. Present Key Performance Outcomes	**2. Evidence Base**
• Modern apprenticeship course prepares students for further education in sport-related courses. • Work-experience opportunities in the PE department allow students to develop the skills required in the workplace. • Involvement in the delivery of A-level PE and BTEC Sport at shared sixth form prepares students for further education and/or work in sport-related areas.	• Coursework completed and student interview. • Student evaluations and student interview. • Course results and student interview.
3. Summary of Strengths and Weaknesses **Strengths** • Modern apprentices developing their teaching/coaching skills while students benefit from having additional teaching staff in lessons. • PE staff gaining experience in the delivery of A/S-level Physical Education course. • Development of students' organisational and interpersonal abilities through Sports Leadership courses and through responsibilities given to team captains in all activity areas. **Weaknesses**	**4. Actions Already Taken to Improve**
5. Future Targets (Learning Outcomes)	**6. Future Actions to Achieve Targets**

An Example Reflecting a Whole School SEF

How does your curriculum area contribute to learners preparing for their future economic well-being?

1. Present Key Performance Outcomes • Students are given opportunity in Years --/-- to take part in work-based activity. Placements monitored. Tutors assess the quality of the work with both students and employers. • The majority of learners leave with a satisfactory level of competency in the basic skills. • Vocational studies available to support non-academic pupils. • High-profile staff appointed who can guide students. • Year 8 pupils complete a unit on banking/dealing with finances/completing applications, in preparation for adult life. Evaluations show that this unit is appreciated.	**2. Evidence Base** • Recruit – staff to teach... • Further develop LSA role. • Develop range of business partners to support shortage areas.
3. Summary of Strengths and Weaknesses • Recruit – staff to teach... • Further develop LSA role. • Develop range of business partners to support shortage areas.	**4. Actions Already Taken to Improve** • CPD/Resource deployment/ Policies/Teaching. • LSAs work in small groups with students to provide support students. LSAs trained in careers support. • Businesses targeted – staff-shortage difficulties in accommodating students/providing mentors. • School staff trained as mentors.
5. Future Targets (Learning Outcomes) • Increase the number of vocational subjects studied to X. • Target students undertaking vocational courses to achieve 65% A–Cs.	**6. Future Actions to Achieve Targets** • Recruit – staff to teach... • Further develop LSA role. • Develop range of business partners to support shortage areas.

4f On the basis of your evaluation, what are your key priorities for development?

• Develop Assessment for Learning resources.

• Improve performance in written examinations in GCSE PE and Dance.

• Develop knowledge and understanding of health and fitness issues through use of the fitness suite.

• Update of programmes of study – football and netball.

Please enter grade. To guide judgement, please consult grade descriptions in the Guidance for Inspectors of Schools.

	Outstanding	Good	Satisfactory	Inadequate
Learners' personal development and well-being		X		

5. The Quality of Provision

To help you focus your comment and judgements in completing this section, please consult the relevant pages in the 'Guidance for Inspectors of Schools'.

Your evaluation of the quality of provision should take account of the **impact** on the standards achieved and the personal development and well-being of learners.

In answering the following questions, please make clear the main evidence, such as monitoring of teaching, on which your evaluation is based.

5a How good is the quality of teaching and learning?

• How well teaching meets the needs of the full range of learners and course requirements.

• The suitability and rigour of assessment in planning learning and monitoring learners' progress.

• The diagnosis of, and provision for, individual learning needs.

• The involvement of parents and carers in their children's learning and development.

1. Present Key Performance Outcomes

- High-quality teaching in the subject area motivates students to participate in curricular and extra-curricular activities. All teachers have excellent subject knowledge.
- Continued high level of attainment in GCSE PE results.
- Positive residuals for all staff teaching at GCSE level (on average, students achieve 0.5 of a grade higher than national average in this subject area).
- Ofsted reports and departmental review – all lessons graded satisfactory or above, plus examples of excellent teaching seen in PE and Dance.
- Enhancement of core curriculum work in extra-curricular sessions.
- All students are assessed in each activity area in which they participate. These assessments are used to inform planning and form the basis of reports to parents.
- GCSE PE practical assessments are agreed by external moderators.

2. Evidence Base

- Teachers' commitment to preparing/planning lessons to a high standard and using a range of teaching styles to enhance inclusion for all – record books, programmes of study, lesson observation.
- GCSE results – Relative Performance Indicator significantly positive over a six-year period.
- GCSE PE analysis and PANDA information.
- Previous Ofsted reports and review documentation.
- Observation of extra-curricular work and achievements of G&T students at higher levels of performance (eg District/County representative).
- Student assessment records.
- GCSE PE results and moderators' reports.

3. Summary of Strengths and Weaknesses

Strengths

- Teaching staff have high expectations of their students.
- Differentiation by task, outcome and use of a range of equipment allows all students to experience success and enhances their enjoyment of lessons.
- Students given responsibility for their own learning (eg planning and leading warm-up, Sports Leadership, reciprocal teaching).
- Students' self-assessments completed after each block of activity.

Weaknesses

- Amount of paperwork generated by assessment system.
- Students' need to be more aware of what they must improve in order to achieve the next level in each activity area.

4. Actions Already Taken to Improve

- Assessment information computerised.
- Increased use of ICT in lessons (eg Dartfish system in practical lessons, ACTIVstudio CD-ROM in GCSE PE).
- 'Global' assessment grade for games activities rather than individual grade for each games activity covered.

5. Future Targets

(Learning Outcomes)

- Students are aware of their targets for improvement of their performance in each activity area.

6. Future Actions to Achieve Targets

- Development of resources for Assessment for Learning.

An Example Reflecting a Whole School SEF

How good is the quality of teaching and learning?

1. Present Key Performance Outcomes

- 100% teaching is satisfactory and 20% is good or better.
- There is a range of satisfactory/good teaching within and across all year groups (1, 3, 5, 10).
- The best teaching can be found in year – and pupils make better-than-expected progress in relation to their targets (1, 4).
- Average-attaining pupils make sound progress. SEN pupils often achieve well. Where teaching is satisfactory, higher attainers are not supported to make the progress they should (1, 2, 10, 11).
- Pupils make at least satisfactory progress in a range of subjects, including Ly/Ny (3, 4, 5, 6, 7, 8, 9, 10, 11).

2. Evidence Base

- Lesson observation records (1).
- Staff-meeting record of training activities (2).
- Summary of work scrutinies in writing, mathematics, history and ICT (3).
- Pupil targets (4).
- Coordinator monitoring records (5).
- PM – training needs (teachers + LSAs) appendix (6).
- Pupil interviews (7).
- Displays (8).
- LA monitoring (9).
- End-of-unit assessments (10).
- Pupil self-assessment (11).
- Marking of pupils' work.
- Sharing good practice ASTs (12).

3. Summary of Strengths and Weaknesses

- All teaching is satisfactory, but we want to raise the amount of good/better teaching.
- SEN pupils achieve well.
- Teachers are committed and willing to undertake training to improve.
- Pupils' views are that they learn effectively.
- Where teaching is good, pupils are motivated and keen to learn. Teaching provides realistic challenge for all. Assessment is thorough. Planned activities for higher attainers consistently meet pupils' needs.
- Where teaching is satisfactory, teachers have secure knowledge of subjects and use learning objectives to plan their work.
- Relationships with adults are constructive and most pupils achieve as expected. Homework complements class work but is not always completed effectively.
- Assessment and use made of it to inform learning is satisfactory. Advice to learners is sound and enables them to achieve in line with expected.
- Teaching assistants are not always used effectively to support individuals, particularly more able, to take a full part in lessons.
- Guidance and support for parents and carers is uneven.

4. Actions Already Taken to Improve

CPD/Resource deployment/ Policies/Teaching

- Whole staff INSET on effective T/L strategies and offer opportunities for staff to observe good teaching in school and that of lead teachers (2, 5, 12).
- Developed a package of training on Assessment for Learning (10, 11).
- Provided opportunities for teaching assistants to develop their ICT skills (5, 12).

5. Future Targets
(Learning Outcomes)

- Raise the quality of teaching – 50% good or better.
- Teachers have better understanding of appropriate level of challenge for all groups.
- Attainment of higher achievers improved by 10%+ in 2005 tests.
- Improved support from parents and carers supports pupils to complete homework tasks.
- Teacher assessments are used to inform planning.

6. Future Actions to Achieve Targets

- Teaching and learning policy agreed. Staff INSET, observations of ASTs, leading teachers, shared practice.
- Paired observations of good/better teaching. LEA consultant support.
- Teaching assistants support individuals/groups of pupils in lessons. Training to help pupils access the wide range of technology (more able – greater autonomy) available in lessons – ICT support/training.
- Develop a programme of activities to engage the support of parents in their child's learning. Parents evenings to explain methods/share understanding of what is required.

5b How well do the curriculum and other activities meet the range of needs and interests of learners?

- The extent to which the curriculum or activities match learners' needs, aspirations and capabilities, building on prior attainment and experience.
- How far the curriculum meets external requirements and is responsive to local circumstances.
- The extent to which the provision enables and encourages learners to be healthy and stay safe.
- The extent to which learners have opportunities to develop enterprise, financial skills and work in teams.
- The extent to which enrichment activities and, where appropriate, extended services contribute to learners' enjoyment and achievement.
- Where appropriate, the extent to which employers' needs are met through developing work-related skills.

1. Present Key Performance Outcomes

- Opportunities for a broad experience in games, athletics, gymnastics and dance at Key Stage 3. Extended opportunities at Key Stage 4 in areas such as OAA.
- High participation rates in core lessons and extra-curricular activities.
- Large number of students selecting PE and Dance at GCSE level over past five years.
- National Curriculum levels attained are commensurate with, or better than, those expected for their age for the vast majority of students.

2. Evidence Base

- Timetable/curriculum manager.
- Class registers and extra-curricular participation records.
- Curriculum manager.
- Student assessment records.

3. Summary of Strengths and Weaknesses

Strengths

- Breadth and balance of activities covered.
- 'Dartfish' ICT package – improves students' ability to evaluate their own and others' practical performance and gives instant feedback.
- Year 11 options programme – highly motivational package of activities – high levels of participation, plus students work with a range of instructors and coaching staff in the local community.
- Mixed-gender dance lessons during Year 7 and Year 8 – develop students' movement skills and aesthetic appreciation.

Weaknesses

- Levels of attainment in tennis.
- Year 7 swimming provision.
- Lack of facilities for fitness training work at Key Stage 4.
- Current programmes of study may not take account of improved standards of performance at Key Stage 2.

4. Actions Already Taken to Improve

- Short tennis embedded into the Year 7 indoor games programme of study.
- Football introduced to the girls' games curriculum at Key Stages 3 and 4.
- Year 9 girls' programme of study altered to include dance and fitness activities.
- Purchase of SAQ equipment to address fitness issues and to add variety to warm-ups for games activities.
- Update of basketball and hockey programmes of study.

5. Future Targets

(Learning Outcomes)

- All Year 7 non-swimmers and weak swimmers identified and will attend a block of lessons at school.
- Students at Key Stage 4 will develop their knowledge and understanding of health and fitness issues through the use of equipment in the fitness suite.
- Football and netball programmes of study updated.

6. Future Actions to Achieve Targets

- Year 7 pupils all attend swimming assessments; weak and non-swimmers identified.
- All Year 10 students will complete a block of work in the fitness suite.
- Year 11 students will be able to select a fitness training option, which will be based in the fitness suite.
- Healthy lifestyle display.
- Review of football and netball programmes of study.

5c How well are learners guided and supported?

- The care, including as appropriate integrated day care, advice, guidance and other support provided to safeguard welfare, promote personal development and make good progress in their work.
- The quality and accessibility of information, advice and guidance to learners in relation to courses and programmes, and, where applicable, career progression.
- The extent to which the school and any additional services contribute to the learners' capacity to be healthy, including vulnerable groups, such as looked-after children.

1. Present Key Performance Outcomes • Students' positive attitudes while in the subject area – enthusiasm and high rates of participation evident in every lesson. • Continued improvement in GCSE results and positive residuals. • Safe working practices mean that there are relatively few injuries in PE lessons and first-aid assistance is always on hand. • Allowances made for individual circumstances (eg PE kit, highlighting success at all levels of ability, alterations made to an individual's curriculum as appropriate).	**2. Evidence Base** • Lesson observation, class registers, pupil interviews. • Data from school and LPSA questionnaires. • GCSE results analysis. • Accident forms and first-aid certificates. • Lesson observations, staff record books.
3. Summary of Strengths and Weaknesses **Strengths** • Students are placed in challenging situations but the teaching staff help them to succeed with this. The success they gain adds greatly to their self-esteem and their self-confidence. • Good relationships between staff and students are clearly evident. • Sports Leadership courses – 'Dreams and Teams' – promoting personal development, communication, organisational skills.	**4. Actions Already Taken to Improve** • Mentoring programme for G&T students and those who are at risk of underachieving in the subject area.
5. Future Targets (Learning Outcomes)	**6. Future Actions to Achieve Targets**

5d On the basis of your evaluation, what are your key priorities for development?

- Development of resources for Assessment for Learning.
- Develop knowledge and understanding of health and fitness issues through use of the fitness suite.
- Review football and netball programmes of study.
- Year 7 swimming provision.

Please enter grades. To guide judgement, please consult grade descriptions in the 'Guidance for Inspectors of Schools'.

	Outstanding	Good	Satisfactory	Inadequate
Quality of teaching and learning:		X		
Quality of the curriculum and other activities:	X			
Quality of care, guidance and support for learners:		X		

6. Leadership and Management

To help you focus your comment and judgements in completing this section, please consult the relevant pages in the 'Guidance for Inspectors of Schools'.

Your evaluation of leadership and management should take account of their **impact** in terms of the outcomes for learners and the quality of provision.

In answering the following questions, please make clear the main evidence on which your evaluation is based.

6a What is the overall effectiveness and efficiency of leadership and management?

- How effectively leaders and managers at all levels set **clear direction** leading to improvement and promote high quality of integrated care and education.
- How effectively performance is **monitored and improved** to meet challenging targets through quality assurance and self-assessment.
- How well equality of opportunity is promoted and discrimination tackled so that all learners achieve their potential (ie inclusion).
- The adequacy and suitability of staff, specialist equipment, learning resources and accommodation.
- How effectively and efficiently resources are deployed to achieve value for money.
- How effectively links are made with other providers, services, employers and other organisations to promote the integration of care, education and any extended services to enhance learning.
- The extent to which governors (and, if appropriate, other supervisory boards) discharge their responsibilities.

- Departmental and Sports College targets met.

- Challenging performance-management targets set and achieved.

- Positive attitudes permeate through all teaching staff to the students.

- Staff are given opportunities to take responsibility for and drive forward new initiatives, and are encouraged to develop provision in areas of particular interest.

- All students are given the opportunity to experience success in the subject through the use of a variety of teaching styles and differentiated tasks.

- The staff are all Physical Education specialists and the department work together as an effective team.

- GCSE PE students continue to achieve at a high level.

- Roles and responsibilities are clearly laid out.

- Use of assessment information when deciding on student groupings, in order to allow every student the opportunity to succeed.

- Use of departmental self-evaluation to identify areas of success/weakness and link findings to CPD needs as well as each individual's performance-management targets.

- Performance-management targets link into PE and Sports College development plans.

- Effective use of all the excellent PE facilities and accommodation.

- Effective links with outside agencies – coaching support, Year 11 off-site options programme.

- Departmental capitation is used effectively to enhance provision for students.

- Link governor involved in departmental self-evaluation.

6b On the basis of your evaluation, what are your key priorities for development?

- Use of department meeting time to further enhance teaching and learning as well as disseminate information.

Please enter grades. To guide judgement, please consult grade descriptions in the 'Guidance for Inspectors of Schools'.

	Outstanding	Good	Satisfactory	Inadequate
Effectiveness and efficiency of leadership and management:		X		

7. Overall Effectiveness and Efficiency

How effective and efficient is the provision of education, integrated care and any extended services in meeting the needs of learners, and why?

To answer the questions raised in this section of the form, you should draw together your evaluations in the previous sections.

To help you focus your comment and judgements in completing this section, please consult the relevant pages in the 'Guidance for Inspectors of Schools'.

In answering the following questions, please in each case make clear the main evidence on which your evaluation is based.

7a What is the overall effectiveness of the provision, including any extended services, and its main strengths and weaknesses?

Overall effectiveness of provision is good.

Evidence:
- GCSE results in PE and dance over five-year period.
- Participation records.
- Extra-curricular provision and participation.
- National Curriculum levels attained and conversion rates between levels.
- SMT review.
- Ofsted reports.
- Students enjoy their lessons and want to succeed.
- Meeting targets – PE department development plans and Sports College development plans.

Strengths:
- High-quality teaching and learning (Ofsted, HMI visit, SMT departmental review).
- Broad and balanced curriculum.
- Extra-curricular provision.
- Staff commitment and ability to work as a team.
- A number of highly experienced staff who are excellent role models.

Weaknesses:
- Facilities (NOF3 building programme and BSF will address this issue).
- Programmes of study need to be reviewed to reflect higher standards being produced at Key Stage 2.
- Year 7 swimming provision.

7b What is the effectiveness of any steps taken to promote improvement since the last inspection, and as a result of your self-evaluation?

- Improved ICT opportunities – Dartfish, GCSE revision package – contributed to GCSE PE and Dance results at an all-time high in 2004.
- Alterations made to girls' curriculum at Key Stage 3 led to an increase in girls' participation in core PE and extra-curricular activities.
- Success of Year 10 fast-track PE group.
- Recognising achievement in sport/PE (Celebration Evenings, Sports Awards Evening).
- Use of AST to support/develop the delivery of Dance at Key Stages 2 and 3.
- Increased use of coaching staff, ITT and modern apprentice students to support teaching staff in the delivery of lessons/extra-curricular activities.
- Assessment system in place, which allows pupil progress to be closely monitored and intervention strategies put in place whenever necessary.

7c What is the capacity to make further improvement?

- Review of programmes of study to reflect increased attainment at the end of Key Stage 2.
- Improved teaching and learning through the development of Assessment for Learning (Key Stage 3 Strategy).
- Improved performance in written exams at GCSE level in PE and in Dance through enhanced ICT provision and further development of teaching materials and resources.
- Development of programme of study for AQA Vocational GCSE in PE.
- Develop teaching and learning links (kinaesthetic learning) between sport and science.

7d How effective are links with other organisations to promote the well-being of learners?

Effective links created to other organisations that promote the well-being of our students. For example:
- School/club links – many students have developed the skills and the confidence to attend a wide variety of sports clubs in the community.
- Sports Leadership – exchange links with Poland, organisation of junior school sports festivals, effectively developing leadership and interpersonal skills.
- Year 11 'off-site' options programme – increases students' awareness of opportunities to take part in sport in the community.
- Health and hygiene talk – Year 7 and Year 10 girls – improved awareness of health issues and increased participation in lessons.

7e What steps need to be taken to improve the provision further?

- Completion of NOF3 building programme, which will enhance changing facilities, allow increased access to ICT in theory lessons for GCSE, BTEC and A/S-level students, and develop awareness of health and fitness issues with the provision of a fitness suite.

7f Where relevant: what are the effectiveness and efficiency of the sixth form? *Not relevant.*

Please enter grades. To guide judgement, please consult grade descriptions in the 'Guidance for Inspectors of Schools'.

	Outstanding	Good	Satisfactory	Inadequate
Overall effectiveness		X		
Capacity to make further improvement		X		
Improvement since the last inspection		X		

References

ACCAC (2000) *Exemplification of Standards in Physical Education Key Stages 1–3: Consistency in Teacher Assessment*. Thames Ditton, Surrey: ACCAC Publications. ISBN: 1-86112-268-3.

baalpe (2004) *Achieving Excellence: Subject Leader in Physical Education*. Second edition. Leeds: Coachwise Solutions. ISBN: 1-902523-57-1.*

baalpe (2005) *Assessment for Learning in Physical Education*. Leeds: Coachwise Business Solutions. ISBN: 1-902523-79-2.*

baalpe (2006) *A Guide to Self-review in Physical Education*. Leeds: Coachwise Business Solutions. ISBN: 1-902523-98-9.*

DfES (2004) 'High Quality Physical Education and Sport for Young People'. March. Ref: PE/HQ.

DfES (2005) 'A New Relationship with Schools: Improving Performance through School Self-evaluation'. DFES-1290-2005.

DfES (2005) 'Do You Have High Quality Physical Education and Sport in Your School?' January. Ref: PE/HQSE.

DfES (2005) 'Every Child Matters: Framework for the Inspection of Children's Services'. July. Ref: HMI 2433.

DfES (2005) 'Every Child Matters: Framework for the Inspection of Schools in England'. July. Ref: HMI 2435.

DfES (2005) 'National PESS Professional Development Programme Modules PD/Q and SD/Q: Evaluate to Inform and Improve'.

DfES (2005) 'School Evaluation Form'.

DfES/QCA (1999) The National Curriculum Handbook for Primary Teachers in England: Key Stages 1 and 2. Ref: QCA/99/457.

DfES/QCA (1999) The National Curriculum Handbook for Secondary Teachers in England: Key Stages 3 and 4. Ref: QCA/04/1374.

DfES (2005) 'The National PESS Professional Development Programme PD/H and SD/H: Assessing Progress and Attainments in PE'.

Ofsted Direct, Issue 4. Autumn term 2005/06.

Ofsted (1998) 'School Evaluation Matters'. Ref: HMI 235.

Ofsted (2000) 'Inspecting Subjects 3–11: Physical Education'. June. (pp 88–92).

Ofsted (2001) 'Inspecting Subjects 11–16: Physical Education with Guidance on Self-evaluation'. May. Ref: HMI 258.

Ofsted (2001) 'Inspecting Subjects Post-16: Physical Education with Guidance on Self-evaluation'. June. Ref: HMI 318.

Ofsted (2005) 'A New Relationship with Schools: Improving Performance through School Self-evaluation'. March.

Ofsted (2005) 'Every Child Matters – Framework for the inspection of schools in England from September 2005'. July. Ref: HMI 2435.

Ofsted (2005) 'Guidance for Inspectors of Schools: Using the Evaluation Schedule'. Ref: 2504.

Ofsted (2005) 'Guidance for Inspectors of Schools: Conducting the Inspection'. March. Ref: HMI 2502.

Ofsted (2005) 'Guidance on the Use of Evidence Forms'. July. Ref: HMI 2505.

Ofsted (2005) Interpreting Data (CD-Rom). April.

Ofsted (2005) 'Self-evaluation Form'. www.ofsted.gov.uk

Ofsted (2005) 'Self-evaluation Forms: Writing a SEF that Works'. July.

Ofsted (2005) 'The Annual Report of Her Majesty's Chief Inspector of Schools 2004/05: Physical Education in Primary Schools'. October.

Ofsted (2005) 'The Annual Report of Her Majesty's Chief Inspector of Schools 2004/05: Physical Education in Secondary Schools'. October.

Ofsted (2005) 'Training for School Inspection 2005: Data Module'. August.

QCA DVD materials or ACCAC video materials on National Curriculum Levels at Key Stages 1, 2 and 3.

QCA (2004) 'The Impact of Self-evaluation on Pupils' Achievement of High Quality Outcomes in PE and School Sport'.

Websites

afPE (formerly PEA UK): Professional Development Record, obtainable from www.afPE.org.uk

DfES: www.dfes.gov.uk

Ofsted: www.ofsted.gov.uk

QCA: PESS website, www.qca.org.uk/pess

Further Reading

Ofsted (2000) 'Education Inequality: Mapping Race, Class and Gender'. Ref: HMI 232.

Ofsted (2000) 'Evaluating Educational Inclusion'. Ref: HMI 235.

Ofsted (2000) 'Improving City Schools: Strategies to Improve Inclusion'. Ref: HMI 222.

Ofsted (2000) 'Sports Colleges: The First Two Years – Innovation in PE and Sport'.

Ofsted (2001) 'Improving Attendance and Behaviour in Secondary Schools'. Ref: HMI 242.

Ofsted (2001) 'Inspecting New Developments in the Secondary Curriculum 11–16 with Guidance on Self-evaluation'. Ref: HMI 262.

Ofsted (2001) 'Providing for Gifted and Talented Pupils: An Evaluation of Excellence in Cities and Other Grant-funded Programmes'. Ref: HMI 334.

Ofsted (2001) 'Managing Support for the Attainment of Pupils from Ethnic Minority Groups'. Ref: HMI 326.

Ofsted (2002) 'Good Teaching, Effective Departments'. Ref: HMI 337.

Ofsted (2003) 'Good Assessment in Secondary Schools'. Ref: HMI 462.

Ofsted (2005) 'The PE, School Sport and Club Links Strategy'. July. Ref: HMI 2397.

*Available from Coachwise 1st4sport. For a full range of sports education and training resources, please visit www.1st4sport.com or call 0113-201 555.